STONEFIELDS

BY THE SEASONS

To my wonderful husband Barry, who enriches my life at Stonefields.

STONEFIELDS
BY THE SEASONS

PAUL BANGAY

With photography by Simon Griffiths

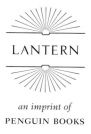

LANTERN

an imprint of
PENGUIN BOOKS

INTRODUCTION

I bought Stonefields in 2005 and moved here the following year. We started photographing the garden as soon as I acquired the property and, in 2013, *The Garden at Stonefields* was published. It told the story of finding and acquiring the piece of land that eventually became known as Stonefields, and the difficulty I had in leaving my previous home, St Ambrose Farm, in the nearby village of Woodend. I talked about my vision for the new house and garden, and followed the development of the property over my first few years here.

That book was produced when the garden was very young – although the hedges were at their mature height, none of the trees or woodland areas were well developed. Gardening is a passion and art form that requires much patience and longterm planning and, years later, there's now a sense of maturity to the garden. The oak trees have not nearly reached their majestic full height, but they do provide scale to the garden and make it feel established. The smaller trees, such as the crab apples and fruiting apples, are all at the height I want them to be, and the pencil pines that guard the front façade of the building are almost too tall.

This makes for a very different book from the first. For a start, my priorities and interests have changed over the years, and these are reflected in the way the garden has developed. I'm becoming mellower with age, as I talk about in the autumn chapter, and that certainly shows in the garden, which is becoming much less formal than I had originally planned it to be. This book will also show how important good soil, drainage and watering are for the creation of a garden. People often comment that the garden looks as if it has been there for decades, but that is all down to those elements, along with the great love and attention it has received. My gardeners, and especially our head gardener, Tim, take great pride and ownership in the garden, and this is also displayed in its rapid and healthy establishment.

Life here is now very different from how it was when I was writing *The Garden at Stonefields*. Living in a mature garden is much more interesting than living in one that is developing from infancy. Instead of spending every spare moment watering, pruning, mulching, planting, weeding, lime washing and constructing, I can now relax and enjoy being in the garden spaces I have created. Many weekends were spent shovelling mulch onto the beds in the heat of summer, and weeding parts of the garden that were yet to receive a protective cover of plant material that deprived the weeds of light and water. It was a rewarding period, but I was much younger and had more energy and flexibility than I do today.

That is not to say there is nothing to do, but what we do now is less strenuous and happens at a more relaxed pace. I still observe the same weekly routine of travelling and working during the week, arriving back at Stonefields for my Friday design day in the studio, which is in the gatehouse. Every Friday morning I get up early, have a light breakfast and travel the same route, up the front stone steps, through the two levels of parterre, past the blue borders, always looking to see what is doing well and what is not. From there, it's into the white garden, where I decide whether to cut across the lawn or take the long route via the pebble path to the gates that separate the main garden from the home paddock.

The last part of the journey is where Ruby, our cocker spaniel, always takes a detour as she plays cat and mouse with our family of magpies. I let her get on with that, and walk down the avenue of large box balls under the driveway oaks and into my studio. It is a well-worn path I often undertake several times a day in order to have morning and afternoon tea and lunch back in the house. This separation between work and living space is important, and the reason why I built my studio a good distance from the house.

Fridays are precious for they're when I get to relax and dream up wonderful schemes for gardens without the distraction of staff, clients or phone calls. The studio is my space, and no-one is allowed in, apart from Ruby and, occasionally, Barry. It's full of all my reference books and archival material, and two walls are covered with inspirational tear sheets from magazines. It's a place for dreaming in and being inspired in and, when I feel depleted, I simply take a walk around the garden and recharge my creative batteries. Sadly, it is not as romantic as Vita Sackville-West's

PAGE 6-7 A drone shot of Stonefields in spring. The main blossom is *Malus floribunda*.

OPPOSITE Box spheres flank the entrance to the twin pavilion in the apple walk, while *Wisteria sinensis* frames the doorway.

writing room in her tower at Sissinghurst, which is a space I often dream of and wish for, but its newness is made up for with its sense of peace and ample space for spreading out.

The weekends are for writing or reading in the main house. In winter, early spring and late autumn, those activities are done in front of the fire in the sitting room. In the warmer months, I retreat to the cool of my desk in our bedroom. It's a cycle strictly adhered to and hasn't changed in the fifteen years since I created Stonefields. In fact, the Friday design day in the countryside has been a part of my life for more than twenty-five years, since designing on the large dining table at St Ambrose Farm.

I enjoy the seasons far more now than I used to. I dread the perilous summers somewhat less than I once did, as we have more shade, and the trees have their roots deep down in the moister subsoil. I relish autumn, with its seasonal colour displayed on a large scale, but still consider winter my favourite time of year – it's when we can all relax and watch the dormant plants sleep away the bitter cold of altitude, and very much look forward to the gush of spring blossom and growth.

New gardens have been added since the last book, including the lilac walk and the twin lower perennial borders below the swimming pool. A number of areas, including the rose garden, have also undergone major change. Many more gardening adventures exist in my mind but, alas, I must stop expanding. Especially for a designer, the downside of owning a more established garden is boredom. I adore creating new garden spaces and experimenting with new forms, planting schemes and structures. Now, the frustration at Stonefields is that there are no more large garden rooms to create. Although a circular terrace has been sculpted into the hill at the far end of the lilac walk, it's begging for a new garden room, and will probably sit empty for many years to come. It's simply rough mown every now and then until some mysterious source of funds appears.

Given the size of the property, I could, of course, keep creating, but I simply couldn't afford to look after it or find the water to irrigate it. One thing that's constantly at the back of my mind is whether to start again somewhere else and enjoy the high that comes from creating a new garden from scratch, or stay here and relax and benefit from all the hard work and effort that has gone into creating this garden. And then there's the perplexing and highly complicated dilemma of what happens when I want to slow down from work. Garden designers never fully retire – two of my heroes, David Hicks and Russell Page, worked right up until they died – but do I need a smaller garden that is easier to look after and that would better suit my financial means when I'm no longer fully employed?

I do dream of a garden with no lawns or hedges; looking after the ones at Stonefields is a constant and time-consuming activity. A smaller garden may be one that is a little jewel, not reliant on scale to create the wow factor. I've written about such gems in my book *Small Garden Design*. I'm sure you could get the same amount of enjoyment from a smaller garden with fewer spaces if those spaces were highly dynamic in their flowering phases and layouts, and relied more heavily on the borrowed landscape view rather than the cultivated. Gravel paths and open spaces could replace water-thirsty lawns, and the odd masonry wall could replace hedges. One thing for sure, I would not line the beds in box hedging, but would design organic-shaped beds, which would allow plants to spill over the gravel and even march forward into the open spaces. Fields of park plantings of hardy trees such as the extremely tough Algerian oak could form a large part of the garden, again requiring little to no water and very little maintenance.

The feelings I have of wanting to move are reduced somewhat by making minor adjustments to existing planting schemes at Stonefields, but these don't compare to the huge high from creating a new garden. I do, of course, create them for clients, and while this is enormously rewarding, there is nothing like your own garden. No other client challenges you more, nor gives you such freedom, which allows you to learn – or forgives the mistakes that experimentation often leads to.

If I were to move, I could never leave this area. I love our part of the world – the Central Highlands of Victoria captured my

heart more than two decades ago. My friends and family are here, and I consider the red volcanic soil my best friend. This is a region rich in history, with intact gold mining towns that have now taken on a life of food, wine and regional art culture. There is so much to do here, which is rare for many parts of regional Australia.

I frequently leave Melbourne bathed in sunshine and, as the highway slowly climbs, the temperature cools and the mist appears, and I know I am in a place I greatly love. It snows in winter, not often but just enough to create magic.

I could not leave the freezing cold winters, the mild springs and autumns and, despite my constant moaning about lack of rain and extreme heat, I have even warmed towards the summers. The highly distinct four seasons are what our region is known for and what I love most. They allow the garden to change radically throughout the year and, as it matures, these changes become more focused and obvious.

I chose to begin this book with autumn because, for me, it's a time to relax and truly enjoy the garden. The stress of summer is over and we can all step back and evaluate and enjoy the way the garden responds to the milder and, hopefully, moister conditions. I can sit in my study, and look out through the windows fringed in a blaze of Boston ivy's autumnal red. The box hedge in the parterre takes on a deeper shade of green, and the apple walk beyond is dripping in produce and colour. I love sitting here and writing; it's the one place in the house that is quiet and offers views in both directions towards the garden. One way looks towards the parterre and the other to the pool borders and distant view of the valley. I purposely designed the house to be mostly one room wide for this very reason – the strong visual connection between the garden and house is vital to the success of both. It's a rare opportunity for complete synergy in design of outdoor and indoor spaces, and came about because the garden design dictated the house design and not, as is often the case, the other way around. I think architects usually have bigger egos than garden designers, and believe the house is far more important than the garden. For me, the garden comes first, and the house must work in tandem with it.

PREVIOUS PAGE
A view from the lower pool borders to the main pool borders. Colour in the foreground is provided by *Salvia nemorosa*, *Geranium* 'Rozanne' and *Penstemon* 'Firebird'.

FOLLOWING PAGE
An obelisk with bronze eagle marks the top of the main axis of the garden. The bird watches over the property, and has been sited to be visible from the sitting room doors.

For now, if not forever, Stonefields is my refuge — it's the place that enriches and relaxes me. As I approach the end of the working week, all I can think about is how long it is before I'm able to get home and see what has happened in the garden in the days that I've been away. We are constantly refusing weekend invitations in the city, as the garden is where we want to be; the time spent there is precious and not to be compromised. To live a life led by the seasons is to live one closely tied to a garden, and Stonefields is mine.

I

AUTUMN

The end of February is officially the tail end of summer but, as all Australians know, the harsh effects of summer can last well into late March and even early April. Every year, the heat and dry of summer seem to start earlier and end later, as we wait for rain that never comes and pray for cool weather. March does bring some relief at Stonefields; due to its mountain elevation, the nights start to get cooler and an occasional dew appears on the morning lawns. The winds that predominantly appear from the north start to shift to the south-west, dying down in their intensity until we finally end up with the calmest season of all, true autumn.

If we are lucky enough to receive some late summer rain, the paddocks – and home paddock, in particular – will turn from golden brown to hints of green. This brings life back into the landscape and minimises the risk of bushfire, which is ever present during the summer. If we don't get rain, the hayed look of summer lasts into late April, and I despair at how the year will eventuate. It seems as if I have spent my entire life talking about and waiting for rain, something that drives all my friends mad.

Autumn is always a huge relief, a time of hope, rejuvenation and change. There's more anticipation around its arrival than for any other season.

The perennial beds are probably at their best in early autumn; after a decade or more of learning the rhythm of their flowering cycles, we have perfected

PREVIOUS PAGE Seasonal colour in the woodland walk.

OPPOSITE Pin oak (*Quercus palustris*) leaves in autumn.

the art of cutting back and extending the time in which those beds flower. The genesis of floral borders in country gardens can be traced back to England, and came about when people wanted to create beds that flowered during the time of year when they enjoyed their gardens the most, namely summer and autumn. They tended not to go to their country estates in winter or, if they did, they wouldn't be spending time in the garden.

As well as appreciating being outdoors in summer, deeply immersed in flowers, we have also come to value what could be considered the skeletal remains of the borders – the seed pods and spent flowers, which extend the life of the beds, looking delicate all the way through autumn, and eerily beautiful in winter, when they capture the frost.

Around Christmastime, we have lots of visitors and mainly entertain outdoors, so it's important that the garden be as full of flowers as possible. Once that's over, we cut back the salvias, penstemons and other spent flowering perennials, which allows them to flush again in early autumn. The timing is critical – if we cut them back too late in the year, the new growth in the spring gets damaged and they will not return to flower. If we leave them altogether, they simply appear dry and withered.

OPPOSITE Autumn leaves of the Washington thorn (*Crataegus phaenopyrum*).

FOLLOWING PAGE
The autumn colours of *Acer truncatum* x *platanoides* 'Pacific Sunset', a type of maple, in the woodland.

MELLOWING WITH AGE

Herbaceous perennials, such as agastaches, salvias, ornamental grasses and achilleas, now play a monumental role at Stonefields, and are of ever-increasing importance. The garden, which is nearly fifteen years old, has matured simultaneously with its creator. When I first designed it, formality, the sculptural nature of hedges and the layering of green upon green were foremost in my mind. As I mellow with age, softness is overtaking my design philosophy, and I'm inviting the blurring of lines into my life.

My youth was so focused and confident, and formality suited this, while at this stage of my life, I'm less demanding and don't require the discipline of organisation and determination. I'm wondering whether this is the reason, or perhaps it may simply be a reaction to the harshness of the world. I have sat back from afar and watched the destruction of my much-loved and often-visited Palmyra, and other ancient cities and monuments, and have lamented the future of man on this planet. Hedges and straight lines don't seem to sit well with this new world, whereas the floriferous informality of perennial borders does.

Whatever the reason, flowers are taking over the garden. The blue borders in the entrance court are continually evolving, but remain true to their original colour palette. In autumn, they're bursting past the confines of their box hedge edging. This edging is also becoming contentious, as I long to see plants spill over onto the paving, not held back by the regimentation of the box. It's very hard, though, to pull out hedges that we have watched growing for years, and have spent countless hours maintaining. We did, however, remove the four crab apples that were in these beds,

as their root system and the shade they created were detrimental to the perennials that now take precedence.

Much of Stonefields is going through this transitional phase; it's a greater challenge as trees mature and create shade, as well as competition for space, soil, nutrition and water. I am ruthless when it comes to removing trees that have been overplanted, or planted in the wrong position, but for some reason, I find it difficult to remove the architectural hedging elements.

For a while, I have been tempted to remove the parterres altogether and replace them with flowering perennials interspersed with organic shapes of clipped greenery. I would probably use *Ligustrum vulgare* 'Buxifolium' instead of box. It's a tougher plant, and not subject to mite attack, as box is. I can imagine it in linear waves, running at angles to the house, weaving in and out of the mass plantings of perennials. No-one agrees with me on this; it would be a massive change, but one that hopefully one day I will find the strength to undertake.

AUTUMN

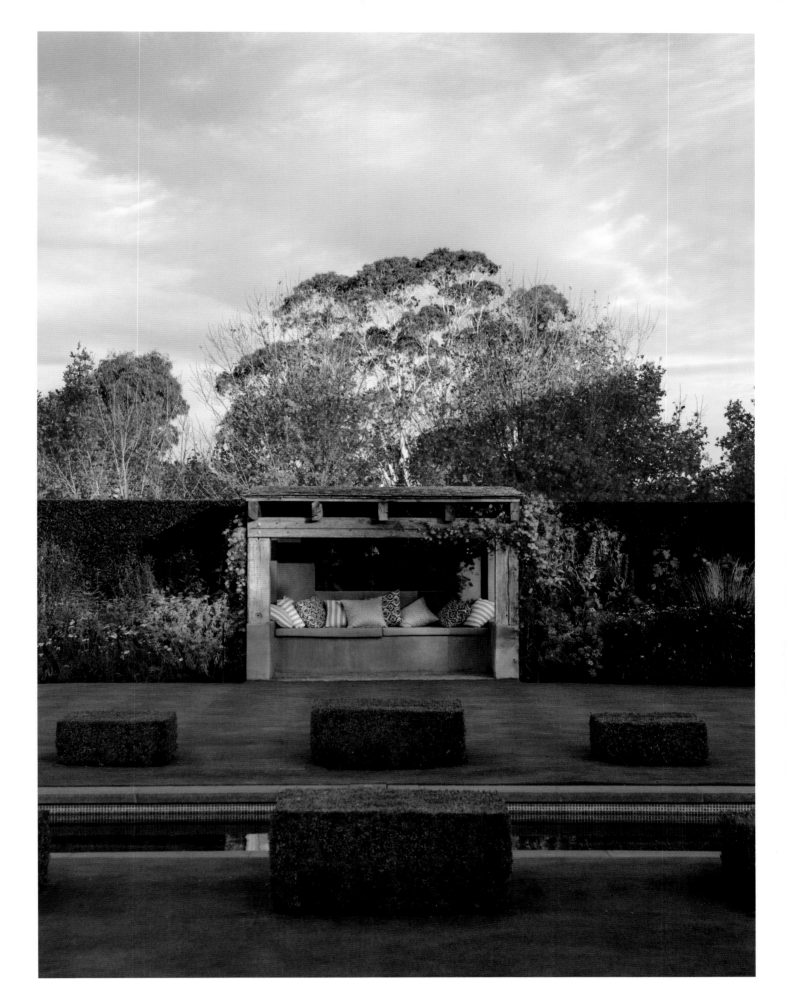

THE FARMHOUSE NEXT DOOR

FOLLOWING PAGE
The farmhouse front garden has a backdrop of ancient eucalyptus trees. In the foreground are the flowering herbaceous borders and a copse of *Malus* x *atrosanguinea* 'Gorgeous'.

PAGE 38 Clipped organic shapes of *Ligustrum vulgare* 'Buxifolium' and arching branches of the smoke bush (*Cotinus coggygria*) in the front garden of the farmhouse.

PAGE 39 Cotinus branches frame a border with *Aster* x *frikartii* 'Mönch', *Perovskia atriplicifolia*, *Dahlia* 'Bishop of Llandaff' and *Calamagrostis* x *acutiflora* 'Karl Foerster'.

I have successfully used *Ligustrum vulgare* 'Buxifolium' as an informal shape in the garden at our farmhouse next door. This building is a new inclusion to Stonefields since the last book, and came into our possession when our neighbour decided she wanted to move. She kindly asked me if I wanted to buy her house, which included another forty-five acres of paddock. My immediate response was to say no, as I didn't need another house. She then very cleverly responded with, 'What happens if someone buys it who rides trail bikes?' I absolutely hate noise in the country; the fear of hearing trail bikes racing around the paddocks immediately led to the purchase of the property.

This initially reluctant decision has proved highly successful – we turned it into a four-bedroomed short-term rental, with guests being offered access to the main garden at Stonefields. That drawcard means we nearly always get garden-loving guests – and, as we all know, they are highly respectful and interesting people to have around.

The house required a new garden as well as a complete makeover. The first task was to render both the inside and outside of the building, transforming it from its very unattractive fake clinker brick skin to the same colour and texture as the main house. This continuity in colour runs throughout the entire property, with houses, pavilions, gate piers and almost all other rendered brick structures limewashed the same chocolate colour. I arrived at this scheme by looking at our soil, which is a deep chocolate red. I thought if we matched the house with it, it would make the house feel as if it belonged to the landscape and simply fade into the background. To me, the garden and the landscape are the main event.

Once we had finished rendering the farmhouse, altered some internal walls, laid seagrass flooring and added new bathrooms and kitchen, it was time to look at the garden. The last thing I wanted was another huge maintenance load for everyone. The garden at the farmhouse just had to feel welcoming and create an introduction to the main garden. We had removed all the foliage that had grown right up to and engulfed the house, and the next thing to do was add a large gravel forecourt, surrounded by deep beds of herbaceous perennials, such as *Salvia nemorosa*, *Sedum telephium* 'Matrona', dahlias and phlomis. This had the bonus of opening up the previously hidden view of the nearby hill and setting sun.

Beyond the perennial beds, I planted a crab apple lawn, consisting of thirty *Malus* x *atrosanguinea* 'Gorgeous', which are high-grafted to both allow guests to run under them and to make for easy mowing access. The rear garden consists of a terrace and small wisteria-covered pergola, leading onto a lawn, again bordered with deep perennial beds. The beds are easy to look after, providing months of flowering colour, and are used to create rooms without the need for hedges. The only hedge we have is an *Osmanthus heterophyllus* 'Purpurea', surrounding all four sides of the garden. I chose this because, unlike the ligustrum in the main garden, it needs very little pruning. On top of that, it's very spiky, which deters the inquisitive cattle that wander out of the surrounding paddock and try to graze in the garden.

THE POOL BORDERS

OPPOSITE Reading
lounges, shaded under
a pergola of *Vitis coignetiae*,
look out to the swimming
pool over a low hedge of
Cotoneaster horizontalis
and the flower heads of
the ornamental grass
Calamagrostis x *acutiflora*
'Karl Foerster'.

FOLLOWING PAGE
The pool borders are
just beginning to fade
in the long shadows of
the autumn sun. The
pool is flanked by cubes
of English box (*Buxus
sempervirens*).

PAGE 44–5 The pool
borders, looking to one of
the twin pavilions, which is
covered in *Rosa* 'Mermaid',
Rosa 'Crépuscule' and
Clematis 'Golden Tiara'.

Back in the main garden, the swimming pool borders come into their own during summer and autumn. During these seasons, and particularly in autumn, the colour scheme is designed to merge with the warm golden tones of the outer paddocks. The golden brown of the ornamental grasses, the fluffy seed pods of the *Clematis* 'Golden Tiara' over the pavilions, the rich rust tones of the macleaya and the seed heads of the thalictrum tone perfectly with the burnt grass on the hills beyond. One perennial I really enjoy in autumn is the sanguisorba, with its sprays of cranberry red flowers. It's so ephemeral and light, and dances in the wind, way above the height of the other perennials.

The pool borders have been expanded over the years both in terms of diversity of species and, physically, in the depth of the beds. When I'm designing garden beds, I nearly always have to remind myself to make them as deep as possible. It's hard to do in the confines of city spaces but, with the luxury of space in the countryside, depth is essential. I made the mistake of first creating the pool beds at 3 metres deep, which we have now increased to 4 metres. As I've learnt on my many trips to England, when you first lay out a garden bed, especially one with a hedge as a backdrop, it looks much larger than it will appear once the width of a mature hedge develops.

When I visit gardens, I nearly always pace out the depth of elements such as beds. Recent trips to Gravetye Manor, the home of the late, great William Robinson in West Sussex, allowed me to see the creation of a new border at the base of the main garden terrace wall. This bed is 5 metres deep and, over the years, I have watched it slowly being planted with ever-increasing density to much success. The lesson is always to create a bed deeper than you think you need;

it's far easier to do so at the time of creation than later, when irrigation, edging, lawns or paths may need to be changed. To me, a deeper garden bed is always far more appealing than a larger lawn, as it means more layers of plants and more texture in the garden. I constantly wage this battle with clients, especially men, who seem to favour paving or lawn over beds.

A big change to the garden has been the inclusion of a twin lower border below the main pool lawn. At first, the garden ended at the edge of the upper lawn, designed perfectly to give the illusion that it floated in the landscape, with the immediate foreground disguised, and only the distant view of the valley to be seen. The crisp edge of the lawn defined its outer limits, and delineated the cultivated from the uncultivated. It reminded me of the great Italian hillside villas with their crisp formality rising high above the informality of the Tuscan countryside.

As I mentioned in the introduction, a huge problem for designers and creators of their own gardens is boredom and frustration. For me, this is massive. To help relieve it, I sculpted another terrace into the paddock below the pool lawn, approximately 8 metres in width. It was designed not to be seen from the house, in order to maintain the illusion of a floating pool lawn and garden. I needed more space to grow flowers, and to experiment with differing types of plants and planting styles. The terrace contained one bed adjacent to the lawn batter separating the upper and lower gardens. The garden then sloped away to the paddock beyond. We have since created an identical bed with a central lawn, the far bed having been created by the construction of a retaining wall that doubles up as one section of our pool fence.

The twin beds are planted with low-growing red and purple perennials, deliberately chosen because they won't become too tall and block the view of the valley from the house. They are close to, or below, the line we can see from the house, so it's not until you reach the edge of the lawn that the garden below is revealed. After their summer pruning, the perennials flower profusely in autumn, especially the *Salvia nemorosa*, *Penstemon* 'Firebird' and *Geranium* 'Rozanne'.

At one end, these twin beds lead to the hedged space with a dining table and, at the other, to the kookaburra gate, which marks the entrance to the woodland. The hedged dining space provides another outdoor eating opportunity in the garden. Sitting on the very outer edge of the garden, it enjoys the best view of the valley. To provide necessary shade, I planted two Chinese elms in the table. They will eventually grow into natural umbrellas.

OPPOSITE A display of *Penstemon* 'Firebird' at the rear of the lower pool border bed.

FOLLOWING PAGE A view of the lower pool border.

AUTUMN

INTEREST ALL YEAR ROUND

Another extension to the garden has been the addition of the lilac walk just below the woodland and accessed via the kookaburra gate. Over the years, I had seen lilac bushes flourish in the region and decided I must have some. I ended up planting one hundred lilac trees, mostly of the 'Congo' variety, which have been underplanted with two autumn-flowering perennials, *Persicaria affinis* and *Ceratostigma willmottianum*. The persicaria's pink spikes of fluffy flowers contrast beautifully with the haze of small blue flowers on the ceratostigma. They were both chosen because they flower in autumn when the lilac walk is devoid of all other flowering plant material. The persicaria also has foliage that turns scarlet in late autumn, and is a great groundcover, smothering weeds and requiring very little watering and maintenance.

The rose garden, designed to be predominantly a spring and summer garden, also contributes to our autumnal floral show with its small flush of roses and dahlias. Red and, in particular, deep rich claret reds are the preference here; the 'Bishop of Llandaff' dahlias along with the 'Munstead Wood' and 'Pierre de Ronsard' roses contribute in their own way to autumn. The dahlias, especially, are known for their autumn flowering and The Bishop never disappoints, providing masses of flowers that are great for picking and bringing into the house all the way through to winter.

Easter falls in the Southern Hemisphere in autumn, and Michaelmas daisies are synonymous with this holiday. I have managed to find a speckled red and white variety, *Aster lateriflorus* 'Lady in Black', that flowers reliably every Easter. It's a great picking variety, lasting for weeks in a vase, so I fill the house with it at this

OPPOSITE
Persicaria affinis.

PAGE 52 *Vitis coignetiae* over the rear terrace pergola.

PAGE 53 The front façade of the house is covered in Boston ivy (*Parthenocissus tricuspidata*).

time of year. It's important to us that we get as many periods of flowering and show to all parts of the garden as we possibly can. I don't believe any garden should be limited to one season in terms of flowering – we always need to maximise the length of the flowering period to create as much interest as possible throughout the year. Layering is difficult, but is worth the effort, requiring careful planning to make room for plants that flower in different seasons within the one garden bed.

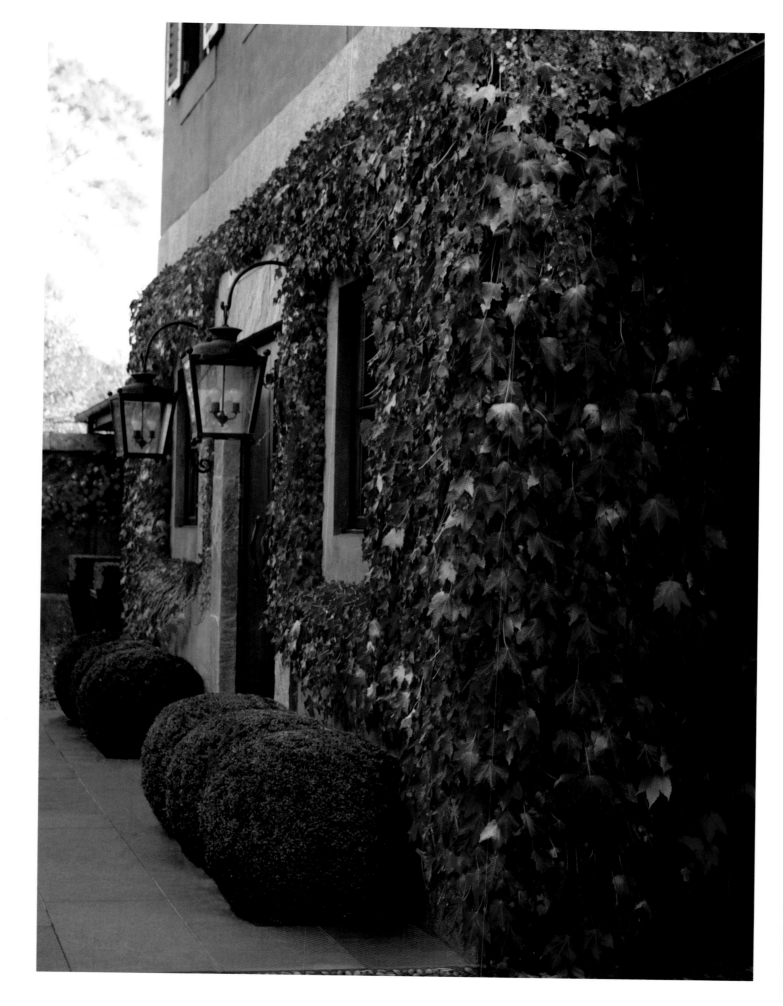

FLOWERS FOR THE HOUSE

The entire garden is used as a playground for flowers to be picked and used to decorate the house – I'm not precious about plundering the garden beds to fill the house with an abundance of flowers. To me, a house with no flowers is an unlived-in house, one that is devoid of a soul. When selecting plants for the garden, my primary motivation is how they will fit with the existing planting scheme in terms of colour, form and texture. Secondary to this is how will they last as a cut flower for the house.

The wonderful part about owning a large garden is that you can rely on different parts of it to supply you with flowers in different seasons. Autumn is the time for dahlias, which are wildly popular at the moment, and for good reason. They last so long as a cut flower, and are incredibly prolific in their flowering. Winter is the hardest time of the year to pick flowers for the house, so I mostly gather bare branches for that purpose. It's a huge bonus if these are covered in lichen that often grows in the wetter colder months. Winter is, of course, the time for hellebores – they carpet the entire woodland, and flower from late winter well into spring. They are tricky as a cut flower, however, because they can droop as soon as you pick them. The secret is to plunge them deep into a container of water straightaway; I carry one with me in the garden. Spring is all about raiding the woodland first; the long branches of the yellow forsythia, which last well indoors, are covered their entire length in golden yellow flowers. The inner circular woodland garden contains boughs of white dogwood and lower plantings of Solomon's seal and thalictrum. The new lilac walk has given me the dream plant for picking, and planting them on such a scale means that in late spring

OPPOSITE *Dahlia* 'Bishop of Llandaff'.

the house is filled with armfuls of lilac flowers with their wonderful and distinct sweet perfume. Summer means roses, and I always fill smaller vases with masses of the red 'Munstead Wood' and pink 'Pierre de Ronsard' roses.

I mostly choose single types of plants for each vase, with the exception of roses where I often do mixed varieties in the one container. Nothing is as beautiful as a large vase of the clashing colours of roses. The rear entry to the house is through what I call the flower room, which was largely inspired by the enormous one that my late great friend Kevin O'Neill had at Marnanie, his house at Mt Macedon in Victoria. Kevin was the greatest florist Australia has seen, and set up this room with shelves of vases in all shapes and sizes, deep counters for arranging flowers, and a large deep basin with an overhead sprung hose for ease in filling and washing the vases. I have recreated this on a sightly smaller scale, and lined it with shelves of green crockery I collect for our dining table. I am a bit obsessed with vases, and often return home with many bubble-wrapped ones bought at antique shops or markets. My preference is for antique glass vases either in clear thick or green glass – the thicker the glass the better. The shelves are so full now that we are having to edit out unused vases for newer ones. I'm afraid collecting is in my blood, and I just can't stop myself.

OPPOSITE *Sanguisorba* 'Cangshan Cranberry'.

AUTUMN COLOURS IN THE WOODLAND

It seems that the seasons are starting and finishing much later than they used to. That's not good as far as autumn goes, as a prolonged summer and hot dry start to autumn means less colour in the trees. When I first created the garden, we were guaranteed a regular start to the season and the colour intensity was far greater – now, in a very dry and warm autumn, the leaves can often turn brown without much hint of colour. In areas such as the woodland that are irrigated, the trees fare much better than the ones in the paddocks which receive limited hand watering, so it's the woodland I look forward to the most in autumn. Two species of trees, pin oaks and maples, were chosen for the intensity of their rich vibrant red tones. With the maples, the odd hint of red, creating anticipation, can often last for weeks before the entire woodland suddenly comes alive with tones of red and orange. The combination is magical, with the vibrant light red of the maples and the richer red of the pin oaks. When I planted the woodland, I deliberately overplanted it in terms of numbers of trees, in order to create as much shade as quickly as possible. Now the trees are maturing, I'm gradually removing the ones that are too close to each other – editing is the name of the game. The trees are complemented by the perennial plantings that clothe the ground under them. Most people don't expect autumnal hues from perennials, but the many woodland varieties we have colour beautifully. The Solomon's seal goes a rich butter yellow, and the neighbouring hostas only a slightly lighter yellow. I love watching them turn from these golden tones to the

final browning and retreating underground. By dying down in the autumn, the plant is able to withdraw after the harshness of a hot dry summer it may have just experienced, discard its damaged leaves and emerge refreshed in the spring.

COOL WEATHER AT LAST

May is the month when the cool weather finally reliably arrives, with a gust of freshness and, for us, a huge sense of relief. The house paddock with its drive of oak trees and serpentine hawthorn hedges comes back to life – it only takes a small amount of rain to green the grass and freshen the hedges and trees. We don't irrigate this part of the garden, but allow it to dry off in the summer months, starting in either November or early December. Many Australians love the hayed off appearance of golden grass in summer, but for me it represents the risk of fire and stress to my much-loved trees. I have, however, come to accept it as another seasonal cycle of the garden, but do love it when autumn comes, and we return to the verdant field of green.

I planted the serpentine tapestry hedge with as much diversity as possible in order to provide drama in each season, and it responds wonderfully to the cool and wet of late autumn. The hawthorns change to a brilliant red and yellow, with some varieties smothered in red berries. The evergreen lonicera goes a slightly yellow tone, while the leafless branches of the rugosa roses are festooned with red rosehips. Inspired by the hedgerows of England, along with the hawthorn hedges that were the early fences in our district, this hedge has been a highly successful addition to the garden.

After a stressful week in the city, it's so exciting to drive through the gatehouse and be greeted by the hedge in its autumnal colour, with the oaks still in leaf and just a slight hint of yellowing, and the green carpet of the grass alive once again.

OPPOSITE The varied colours and textures of the serpentine tapestry hedge provide an ever-changing backdrop to the obelisk.

FOLLOWING PAGE The main axis of the garden is focused on the front of the house. Boston ivy (*Parthenocissus tricuspidata*) adds vibrant colour in autumn.

AUTUMN

THE START OF TULIP TIME

One of my favourite activities happens in May — the planting of all the spring-flowering bulbs in the old coppers I've been collecting for many years. They're the liners to old washing tubs, and come in a variety of sizes and degrees of verdigris. The colour varies from pot to pot, and can be anything from a vibrant acid to a dull dark green, and it's this mix in size and colour that makes the collection unique.

I used to find the coppers in shops and antique markets, but they tend to find me now. People who have them, or know where there are some for sale, contact me after seeing them on my Instagram or during open days. Apart from the fact that they are the perfect depth and width for bulbs, are light and easy to move around, and sit beautifully on my new Italian granite paving, what I love about them is their sense of age and the patina created when the copper oxidises with the air.

I select the tulip bulbs in summer from the exciting catalogues that always seem to arrive at a low point in the garden's calendar, when it's looking tired, and it's too hot to go outside and work. Nothing cheers me up more on a summer's day than selecting spring-flowering bulbs. I sit inside the house, sheltering from the heat, with masses of catalogues on my lap, circling the bulbs that catch my attention, and painting a picture in my mind of new colour combinations.

The prized pots of tulips sit in the small side terrace beside the herb garden — from the very early days of the garden, the entire space was designed for the placement of a group of three pots in each corner. I plant somewhere between fifty to

OPPOSITE Trugs of bulbs ready for planting.

FOLLOWING PAGE Ruby watches as I plant the old coppers with tulips.

a hundred bulbs per copper pot in a double row. First, I fill the pot approximately a third full with potting mix, and place half the bulbs, almost touching each other, on top of that. I then add another layer of potting mix, followed by the rest of the bulbs and a good covering of potting mix. The coppers are then well watered and placed in their final position. Despite initially looking empty, the anticipation of what is to follow in early spring more than compensates for that.

Every year, we add more bulbs to each part of the garden. The parterre, which already contains more than 8000 white tulips, is topped up annually as old bulbs perish – the number depends on the previous year's show. Thanks to technology, we can now take a drone photo of the parterre in bloom to reveal gaps in the flowering, which makes it much easier to replant in autumn. The tulip we chose for this purpose is 'Clearwater' – its flowers are just tall enough to clear the box hedge, and it blooms just before the next flush of deep purple 'Queen of the Night' tulips, which are mixed in with them in the parterre.

The rose garden is well on the way to being full of 'Paul Scherer' tulips, but we still find ourselves adding an extra 500 a year. They're deep red plum in colour, which is similar to the colour of the roses that follow, and complement the bronze foliage of the *Anthriscus sylvestris*.

The white garden gets its annual top up of 'Clearwater' and 'Spring Green' white tulips. It doesn't flower as well here as in other parts of the garden, probably due to the competition from the large pleached hornbeams.

We are in the fortunate position of being able to leave our tulip bulbs in the ground, which is all to do with the rare combination of extremely well-drained soil, cold winters and hot dry summers, along with the extra depth we plant the bulbs. In fact, they're so happy, they multiply. I don't think I'd have them in the garden if I had to lift them and replant them every year – it would add too much to the maintenance load.

OPPOSITE *Agastache* 'Sweet Lili' and *Echinops bannaticus* 'Taplow Blue'.

DAFFODILS AND BLUEBELLS

I usually loathe daffodils – they look like fried eggs dotted all over the landscape – but have rather taken a fancy to our farmhouse drive being lined with large drifts of yellow and white ones. When I bought the farmhouse, they were already there, which was no surprise to me as I had witnessed their annual blooming from afar. They are randomly planted under the oak trees on either side of the drive, and every autumn, I plant new swathes of each colour, usually adding 500 of the yellow 'Camelot' and an equal number of white 'Victorious'. The aim is to eventually cover the entire driveway verge in daffodils, which will be quite appropriate for this area. Our local town of Kyneton has an annual daffodil festival, which attracts many visitors – the two main roads into it are lined with tens of thousands of bulbs. This part of the world is now known for bulbs, and in particular, daffodils. Our small drive is a nod to this feature.

A few years ago, I experimented with planting 'Renown' tulips in the blue borders in the entrance court. They did extremely well the first year, but returned with a virus the second one. This may be because the beds receive summer irrigation, and tulip bulbs prefer to be dry at that time of year. The next year, I tried *Allium* 'Purple Rain', which has been highly successful, with the large flower heads floating above the box hedge for many months. I even love them when they have finished flowering in late October to November and are dry round flower heads. We now plant 200 a year in autumn, and it looks like they all survive from year to year.

This autumn, for the first time, we planted thousands of bluebells deep in the centre of the woodland beds, which had

previously been overgrown with low-hanging viburnums and evergreen shrubs. We uplifted the lower foliage of all these plants to leave large areas of bare bed – I'm hoping the bluebells will fill this empty space, and thrive in the shade and summer irrigation. The first time I saw a bluebell wood was when I was staying in the Priest's House at Sissinghurst. This rental cottage has to be one of the greatest holiday destinations for any serious gardener – not only does it sit in the white garden, but you have twenty-four hour access to the whole garden. On a walk one morning, I came across a woodland carpeted in bluebells – the entire scene was a haze of blue lit by streams of sunlight through the trees. I thought it so magical that I was determined that, when I had my own wood, I would fill it with bluebells.

As autumn slowly shifts to winter, the Japanese maples are the last to turn brilliant red. They complement the last of the nearby ornamental grape foliage that drapes over the twin pergolas covering the north terrace of the house. The lilacs, which are not at all spectacular as far as autumn colour goes, are underplanted with a carpet of the vibrant red *Persicaria affinis* and *Ceratostigma willmottianum*. When I planted these two groundcovers, I had no idea about their autumn secret; both are hugely rewarding and tough, requiring very little water and attention.

Right up until the end of autumn, the Boston ivy clings to the lower portion of the house, with the bright red of the leaves intensified by the red limewash of the façade. I love my house being clothed in this climber – it turned a very new looking building into something with character, having the illusion of age and establishment. Boston ivy requires a huge amount of work in the summer, as it practically grows overnight into the windows and eaves, but its green glossy leaf in summer and red autumn tones are just too irresistible.

As the days slowly lose their midday warmth, and the trees, climbers and shrubs lose all their leaves, I know winter is coming. The valley fills with mist that can linger for days, and as the odd day of rain is replaced with days of constant drizzle, winter is definitely on the way.

OPPOSITE
Acer truncatum x *platanoides* 'Pacific Sunset'.

PAGE 78 Washington thorn (*Crataegus phaenopyrum*) hedge.

PAGE 79 Pin oak (*Quercus palustris*).

PAGE 80-1 Boston ivy (*Parthenocissus tricuspidata*) clings to the lower part of the house. Cubes of English box (*Buxus sempervirens*) in timber planters, alongside English box spheres, flank the front door.

Autumn is one of the busiest times in the garden, as all the **PERENNIALS** need to be cut to the ground and, using our own compost, the beds **MULCHED**. The mulch not only protects the plants from the cold winter and hot summers, but also adds much needed organic material to the soil. Often we will also spread some well-rotted manure or other organic fertiliser onto the soil before covering it with the mulch layer of compost. We wait until late in autumn to cut the perennials almost to the ground – this allows for some late flowering and autumn foliage plants to finish their show for the year.

The **BOX HEDGING** gets a light prune to remove the wispy summer growth and restore it to its desired form. We avoid doing the pruning during frost or the last of the summer heat, as this can burn any new foliage that may grow.

All the **TALLER HEDGES** of ligustrum, prunus and laurus receive a light trim. In Europe, all pruning tends to happen in autumn, but we favour a major prune in the spring and light prune in autumn. If you prune in spring, you remove the majority of the new growth. With only minimal new growth occurring in autumn, the light autumn prune sharpens the form of the hedges, and ensures the garden looks crisp all year round.

We have a huge number of deciduous trees at Stonefields, and these are constantly losing leaves during autumn. Raking and removing the leaves to the compost pile is a relentless task, but **COMPOSTING** is one of our greatest joys at Stonefields. Our soil is volcanic and rich, but lacking in organic matter. Adding compost provides this missing ingredient to an otherwise perfect soil. To accommodate the enormous amount of leaf fall, we have three 2.5 metre by 3 metre bays separated by walls of timber sleepers. All our leaf matter, grass clippings and vegetable scraps are placed into these bins and allowed to compost. We rotate them allowing each bin to be at a different stage of composting. After between about three and six months, the compost will be ready to be used as mulch on the garden beds. It's important to keep the compost moist but not too wet, and to turn it over regularly to allow as much air into the rotting matter as possible. Heat, moisture and air are a compost bin's best friends.

Mid to late autumn is the time to **PLANT ALL OUR SPRING-FLOWERING BULBS** in garden beds and pots. Tulips, bluebells, fritillarias and daffodils get planted by the thousands in the ground, while the copper pots are filled with an array of tulips.

OPPOSITE The white garden in autumn. The *Malus spectabilis*, a type of crab apple, is better known for its spring flowers than for its autumn foliage.

Early autumn is the best time to **PLANT TREES**. If that happens as soon as the heat of summer is over, they have time to grow some new roots and prepare themselves for the next spring and summer. We also plant as many shrubs and perennials as possible at this time for the same reason. If it's not possible to plant during the autumn, it can happen up until late winter or maybe very early spring if the weather is not too hot. We always avoid planting in late spring and summer, as trees are more likely to develop heat stress.

With expected rain in autumn or, at worst, winter, autumn is also the time we give our lawns a **TOP DRESS AND SEEDING** to increase their density. It also removes inconsistencies with the soil level. It's important to get some warmth during the daytime for the seed to germinate; sowing seed too late will delay growth until spring or risk losing the seed to frost.

Autumn is a good time to **WALK AROUND** the garden to see what hasn't done well over the summer and needs to be replaced – a garden is not a hospital. If anything is struggling, I always remove it and replace it with something more resilient or appropriate.

AUTUMN

AUTUMN PLANTS

A type of **MAPLE**, *Acer truncatum* x *platanoides* 'Pacific Sunset', planted in the woodland, gives a reliable show of intense red.

PIN OAKS, also in the woodland, have a colour palette in autumn ranging from red to orange. If they haven't burnt in the summer sun, they hold onto the colour the longest of all our autumn trees.

JAPANESE MAPLES are the last of the trees to colour; we only have two and they bookend the rear of the house.

VITIS COIGNETIAE covers the pergolas and rear of the house, and provides the garden with an intense scarlet red.

PARTHENOCISSUS TRICUSPIDATA, or Boston ivy, covers nearly all the walls of the house. After protecting the building from heat during summer, in autumn it turns on the most magnificent show of orange to red foliage.

MALUS TRILOBATA is the best of the crab apples for autumn colour, in shades of red to orange.

QUERCUS RUBRA, or red oak, a very reliable and hardy tree, has large leaves, which turn a deep red during autumn.

COTONEASTER HORIZONTALIS, a low shrub, grows up the north façade of the house. It has a fan shape and in autumn its small leaves turn scarlet.

PERSICARIA AFFINIS and *CERATOSTIGMA WILLMOTTIANUM* colour together under the lilacs in shades of orange and red. The low shrub and groundcover are rare in the fact that they do exhibit autumn colour.

Asters, particularly *ASTER* 'MÖNCH' and *ASTER* x *FRIKARTII* 'JUNGFRAU', are in their prime in the herbaceous borders. We plant them to extend the flowering life of the borders into the autumn months.

EUTROCHIUM MACULATA 'GATEWAY' starts flowering in late summer, but peaks in early autumn. Its large mauve flower heads are carried on tall stems, making it perfect for the rear of the blue borders.

MALUS DOMESTICA 'CRIMSON CRISP' is the fruiting apple variety in the apple walk. In spring it has amazing pale pink flowers, while in autumn the main show comes from its delicious eating apples which, deep red in colour, also look beautiful on the trees.

OPPOSITE *Acer truncatum* x *platanoides* 'Pacific Sunset' lines the meandering woodland path, which leads to a distant view of the valley.

II

WINTER

A lot of Australians detest the winter dormancy exhibited by many cool climate plants, preferring to have evergreens in their gardens. I have frequently heard clients stating that they wouldn't want a 'dead' plant in winter when they can have a perfectly normal one that's green all year round. For me, watching plants that obey each season has a romance attached to it – it's the ability to actually see the universal cycle of life in your own little patch.

Winter, in fact, is my favourite season at Stonefields; it's the one time of the year I can relax and know the garden is in good hands with nature looking after her. No watering is required, there's no threat of bushfire and very little need to mow or trim hedges. The garden beds have all been put to sleep under their protective coat of compost and manure, and are lying dormant until the first warm days of spring.

I can also enjoy the house in winter, often spending endless days inside by the fire, watching the rain and occasional flurries of snow falling outside, catching up on my reading or writing. It's hard to express the enormous sense of satisfaction you get from creating a shelter that protects you from the harsh elements of the weather.

Winters are extremely cold and harsh, thanks to our relatively high altitude of 620 metres. In the mornings, the land is often blanketed in a thick layer of frost, and most years we receive at least a light dusting of snow, and every now and then a heavy fall.

PREVIOUS PAGE
The rose garden in winter, before the roses have been cut back.

OPPOSITE The slate-roofed pavilion on the apple walk. Clouds of English box (*Buxus sempervirens*) provide winter interest.

FOLLOWING PAGE
The blue borders, with all the perennials cut back for winter hibernation.

THE MATTER OF WATER

We receive most of our rain in the winter, which is actually annoying as it is the time we least need it – summer and spring rain would be much better for tree growth. We try to harvest and store as much of this rain as possible, with all the buildings' roofs plumbed to our large 240,000 litre tank. Most years, this will overflow into the paddock below. We use the stored water for the house and garden, but sadly, it is not enough to get us through the summer. A bore has been drilled to top up the tank in the hottest months of the year.

The top paddock was already carved out to channel water into the existing dam, which we have since made larger, so that it sits exactly in the centre of view from the front gate. We don't use this water for anything apart from its rich visual factor. As you come through the front gate, it is framed by pin oaks and the first feature of the property you see. During the winter months, it's so satisfying to find it full to overflowing.

Part of the problem with the dam, though, is our extremely well-draining and deep topsoil. There's no clay, and therefore the dam doesn't hold water for long, which is a constant source of frustration for me. It is always empty by late spring and doesn't refill until we get good winter rain. I've contemplated installing a synthetic liner, which apparently would be reliable, but very expensive. The problem is working out how to disguise that point where the liner meets the ground surrounding the dam.

The trick would be to cover that interface with plenty of soil, and plant water plants in this zone. I dream of this water feature, full the entire year, bordered by water iris and sedges, and maybe the odd gunnera, which all do well on the water's edge

OPPOSITE The white garden under snow.

FOLLOWING PAGE Snow comes infrequently to Stonefields, and is magical when it does.

PAGE 96–7 A dusting of snow sits on the box spheres lining the path to the design studio.

and in our climate. It's a large expense that keeps getting passed on to the next year's budget, but one that will be done eventually. Having a large body of water in any landscape or garden makes the summers bearable and is also good for bushfire protection.

THE GARDEN FROM INDOORS

Being perched on the precipice of a hill overlooking the valley below allows me to experience the weather as it moves across the valley and up towards us. I love nothing more than to sit in front of the fire, watching storm fronts descend on the garden, comfortable in the knowledge that the house is well heated, double glazed and solidly built. Every weekend, I get time to read the many magazines I subscribe to as well as the weekend papers (only the weekend editions with their lifestyle sections will do). As I sit in the same chair, that I fight over with Ruby, I can look right towards the pool and valley beyond, and left to the rill and snake ponds. If it's raining and freezing outside, I couldn't be happier in this position. If it's sunny and mild, though, I feel the urge to get up and walk around the garden, which is a distraction that the many views of it provide.

OPPOSITE The pool garden in the snow.

FOLLOWING PAGE
When it snows, the valley view is obscured.

PAGE 102–3 A view from the house into the woodland. The woodland garden is slightly more protected, thanks to the evergreen shrubs, such as laurel and bay, surrounding it. *Helleborus orientalis* are in flower in the foreground.

MAKING TIME FOR MAINTENANCE AND NEW PROJECTS

OPPOSITE The vegetable garden is less productive in winter, but is still ripe with beetroot and brassicas.

PAGE 106 The leaves of the English oak (*Quercus robur*) often stay on the tree during winter.

PAGE 107 *Rosa rugosa* 'Alba' and the caterpillar hedge. The ligustrum hedge, which divides the white garden from the home paddock, remains evergreen, even during the coldest of winters.

Winter is a time to construct or repair the infrastructure that we don't have time to deal with in the growing seasons. Given the scale of the garden, the irrigation system is very extensive and always in a state of flux. We had to convert from our initial drip to an overhead spray system, which has been a major adjustment for the gardeners, and winter was one of the best times to make this change. The old drip system was ten years old, and had started to block up and become entangled with the roots of the hedges and trees. Coverage became patchy and, as a result, some areas of the garden did well and others didn't; it's often a matter of not knowing which parts are not receiving water until it's too late.

With overhead sprays, you can actually see the water delivery and make sure it is covering the entire garden bed. I know there is a great deal of debate about drip versus overhead sprays, the main argument often being that drip irrigation uses less water. In theory, this is correct, as less water is lost to evaporation, and it is delivered directly into the root zone of the plants. In reality, however, the drip line moves away from plants and blocks up, especially with the calcium we have in our water. As we replace each garden's drip system with overhead sprays, we have seen a marked difference in the health and growth of the plants. That said, we have left the drip system to water hedges in certain areas, such as the ligustrum and prunus. It seems to perform much better when it's running in a perfectly straight line and only irrigating one width of hedge.

We have also irrigated all the pots around the garden, and that's another task we carried out over winter. During summer, it used to take an enormous amount of the gardeners' time to hand water each one. Pots are usually afterthoughts in a garden or, like our tulip pots, may need to be moved regularly, which makes it difficult to install irrigation. I am now, after thirteen years of thought and change, content with the placement and quantity of our pots, so it's possible to connect them to the automatic system. This has saved so much precious summer maintenance.

I have never lived in a garden I created that is more than ten years old. St Ambrose Farm was only eight when I left it to move to Stonefields, and my courtyard garden in inner Melbourne was only three years old. Both were in perfect working order when I left them. Once you pass the ten-year mark, repairs become necessary. Our paving has lifted or broken in places, the render has come off in certain parts of the retaining walls, and the limewash needs retouching on structures around the garden.

As the garden and plants need minimal attention in winter, this is the best time to undertake those repairs. However, that's often difficult to do because of the weather; in midwinter, the daytime temperature rarely exceeds 10 degrees Celsius and can often drop to minus 5 degrees at night. At these temperatures, cement will not cure, and the water pipes can freeze. It's a matter of planning around the cold, but lots can still be done.

It's also the time of the year for new projects, and that usually means new garden spaces. This has happened on a fairly regular basis each winter — we did the farmhouse garden one year, the lilac walk another, and the twin lower pool borders one other year. However, the project doesn't have to be a major one like any of these — it can be as small as making a new border against an outside wall of the rose garden.

These days, I desperately try to resist the temptation to develop new spaces, as the garden is already requiring a huge amount of maintenance. For a designer, this is difficult, as your mind always wants to explore new planting schemes or new spaces.

OPPOSITE Bamboo cloches protect the brassicas from birds.

FOLLOWING PAGE The ligustrum hedges create a walled garden, protecting the plants from the harsh winter winds.

CHANGING MICROCLIMATES

As a garden matures, the microclimate in each space changes drastically, especially when it has been created from a bare paddock, as was the case with Stonefields. At first, all parts of the garden received full sun, and the planting scheme was designed to suit. As the hedges and trees have grown, the garden is experiencing increasingly more shade, which means we have to adapt or, in some areas, completely change the planting schemes.

The white garden is one such space. The original planting scheme of white rugosa roses and perennials started to fail once the pleached hornbeam hedge left it nearly in full shade, so it was time to replace it with a shade-loving scheme. All the roses were removed, and only the veronicastrum and aquilegias were retained, as these both tolerate the new shady conditions. At the rear of the bed, directly under the pleached hornbeams, I have added three different hydrangeas — *Hydrangea paniculata* on the sunnier side, and *Hydrangea macrophylla* and *Hydrangea arborescens* on the shadier sides. To the front of the bed, *Philadelphus* 'Manteau d'Hermine', *Anemone* x *hybrida*, *Carpenteria californica* and Shasta daisies (*Leucanthemum* x *superbum*) have been planted. I am hoping all these will suit not just the shade but also the massive competition from the trees and hedges.

OPPOSITE Terracotta forcing pots for endives.

FOLLOWING PAGE
The bare wisteria branches cloak the central marble statue in the rose garden.

WOODLAND PLEASURES

In late winter, the woodland is full of the promise of spring, with green shoots or flower buds from all the bulbs appearing and the hellebores in full flower. I first planted the woodland with the common pale pink and white *Helleborus orientalis*, which have flourished almost too well, invading all available bare soil. Now, I much prefer the deeper plum and almost black varieties, and seek them out at rare plant fairs. They're far more dramatic and moodier, and I adore picking them for the house.

One star in the woodland at this time of year is the *Chimonanthus praecox* – you would never plant it for its foliage or form, but in winter, insignificant little cream flowers appear that have the most amazing strong and sweet perfume. It permeates the entire woodland, making our morning walks absolute bliss. The plants are near the entrance to the woodland from the house paddock, and to find them, you go through the gate between the mixed hedges of hawthorn, hazel, rugosa rose and two types of honeysuckle. One of these honeysuckles is the winter-flowering variety, which blooms at the same time as the chimonanthus, and their scents are equally strong. You need to be close to the honeysuckle to smell it, so I planted it on either side of the gate. As you brush past it, it releases more of its perfume.

The woodland was the last main part of the garden to be created, and that was in response to the lack of shade in the main garden. I pined for delicate plants that needed a moister and shadier environment, and also felt lost without shady areas to visit. It's important to have both light and dark in a garden – the contrast between them brings it to life. Given the overplanting of trees,

OPPOSITE *Forsythia* x *intermedia* branches.

it didn't take long to achieve shade – the pin oaks and maples were planted in abundance and way too close to each other. My theory had been to create a tight woodland of trees with a dense canopy, imitating a natural woodland and giving us shade reasonably fast.

In reality, as the trees are too close together, we're now slowly having to remove the weaker specimens. Winter is the best time to do this as, without leaves, it's much easier to see their spacing. To make sure the impact is not too great, we remove only a few trees each winter – this also gives neighbouring ones time to fill the gaps. Eventually, the trees will be comfortably spaced, with room for smaller shrubs and plants to grow underneath them.

One of the most captivating encounters with the woodland is from our bathroom, which looks directly up the path towards the circular lawn in the centre of the woodland beds. From the window, you can see the many hellebores in flower and the emerging bluebells. When it snows, you can see it sitting on top of the box spheres flanking the steps, and if you open the window, you get the scent of the chimonanthus. Creating vistas from each window was foremost in my thoughts as I designed both the house and the garden. The woodland was an afterthought to the original scheme, and so there's one flaw in its design, and that's the view from the bathroom, which has a kink in it. The lay of the land meant the centre of the circular lawn wouldn't be directly in the centre of view. I now believe, however, that this adds a certain intrigue to the view. It is a vital part of my design philosophy to allow for views or vistas from within the house. I believe glances you get from inside should lead you out into the garden. For this reason, I often create vista lines and focal points, lining up with the front or rear door or windows.

OPPOSITE I enjoy the parterre the most when it snows; it looks like lamingtons to me.

PAGE 120 The woodland garden, with a dusting of snow.

PAGE 121 Artichokes in the snow.

PAGE 122-3 A snowy scene in the parterre.

SIGNS OF LIFE IN THE GARDEN

I know the end of winter is near when the swallows return from their warmer winter holiday, appearing in late August, just as the nights are shortening and the days are warming. Their return signals life is coming back into the garden after its short winter hibernation. The buds on the forsythia start to swell, and the box plants change from their bronze hues into their vibrant green tones. It's this time of the year that, for me, the garden looks at its best, devoid of most of its floriferous colour, but perfect in both its architecture and structure. There are but a few weeks at the end of winter when I wish I could freeze the garden with all the new growth just starting to flush and nothing needing to be trimmed. It's the calm before the storm of spring growth.

The vegetable garden is the one part of the garden that continues to flourish during winter. The perennial beds, containing asparagus, rhubarb, berries and the like, are cut back and dormant, but all other beds are full of brassicas, lettuce and root crops. We grow brussels sprouts, cabbage, kale and broccoli beautifully in winter, under their arches of bent elm branches supporting blackbird mesh. This protective covering is solely employed to keep Harold the peacock from dining out on the brassica leaves, which he seems to love. The lettuce variety we grow best in winter is baby cos. It doesn't mind the morning frost, and can then be harvested in the afternoon. Unlike most lettuces, where you have to pick the whole plant, with the baby cos you can simply pick as many leaves as you need. Carrots and beetroot grow all year round, but particularly love our rich soil and cold weather. While the rest of the garden is in dormant mode, it's refreshing to have

FOLLOWING PAGE
The rose garden, ready for its winter prune.

PAGE 128 *Helleborus* x *hybridus* 'Plum Purple'.

PAGE 129 Snow clusters in a *Euphorbia* 'Copton Ash'.

one part of it productive and flourishing. Unsurprisingly, it's the most visited area of the garden during winter.

Late winter is our favourite time of the season for walking, and we often do a morning and afternoon lap, taking in the entire garden and front paddock. On every lap, we gather the masses of dropped branches from our eucalyptus trees. The trees are messy, but very useful – we always arrive back at the house with armfuls of kindling, including the one stick that Ruby carries in her mouth.

At this time of year, the surrounding paddocks and inner field that we don't irrigate in summer are healthy and green, and the hedges perfectly neat, just waiting for their huge growth spurt which will render them fluffy and completely out of shape. It's a joy to walk around the garden on a cold frosty morning knowing the ground is moist and no plants are suffering from the extreme heat and dry.

By now, the gardeners have completed the hardscaping, and are gearing up for the onslaught of spring that brings the most work in the calendar year. As we move from the nakedness of winter to the abundance of spring, with the late winter reveal of young green shoots, I am already missing the skeletal form of the garden. The first to show signs of the forthcoming spring is the *Euphorbia robbiae* in the woodland; the curled acid green buds slowly unfold during late August, and are a foil to the stark white flowers of the surrounding hellebores. This euphorbia is a great filler in woodland plantings, as it will grow right up to the tree trunks, in a zone where it is hard to get anything else to thrive. It spreads gently and not invasively, and requires very little summer watering. Around this time, too, all the bulbs have emerged. Some, like the daffodils, are in bud, but have yet to flower. The weather is still reliably cold, with no hint of the warmth to come.

While the plants and lawns are dormant, we have far more time to devote to the **REPAIR** of all infrastructure, including irrigation, paving, walls and buildings. Irrigation is also easier to see and access, as most plants are either cut down for the year or deciduous.

It's recommended that most **PERENNIALS GET DIVIDED AND REPLANTED** every three to four years, but we do it only every five to eight years. I'm sure the plants don't perform as well, but it saves valuable time, and I find they still flower perfectly well for up to eight years. We lift them using a fork or shovel and simply prise them apart, keeping the healthy smaller parts and giving away the rest.

Wet winter days are the perfect time to **REORGANISE** the sheds, and clean and sharpen tools ready for spring. The tools are wiped with a moist rag, sharpened on a grinder and oiled to protect them.

We find winter is a good time for undertaking all our **NEW BUILDS**, including paving, walls, earthworks, paths, and so on. The garden beds and lawn are dormant, so more time can be spent performing these capital works programs.

We're slowly swapping our loose pebble areas for **GRANITE PAVING**. This is laborious work, and winter is the perfect season for carrying out this task. The pebbles are hard to manage, as they move around, need raking and weeds appear through them. Paving is easier for people to walk on and saves on maintenance.

All **PRUNING** of fruit trees, roses and wisteria happens in winter. This has always been the traditional time to prune these plants and trees, as you can see the branch structure without leaves. The late winter pruning also encourages spring growth. All lifting of the lower foliage of trees happens at this time of the year, too. We prune off all lower growth on the trunks of the trees to about 1200 mm and, on the taller trees such as the oaks, up to 1500 mm, both for aesthetic reasons and for easy access for mowers. Capability Brown always up-pruned trees to the height of grazing cattle and it's a look I much admire.

We rarely have to clean our **PONDS** due to the well-balanced ecosystem we have established between fish and water plants. Occasionally, they will need to be emptied and cleaned, and winter is the best time for this.

With their lack of foliage, it's a good time to see what's happening with the trees in the **WOODLAND**. Each year, we remove a few as they mature and start to grow too close to each other.

The insignificant small flowers of the *CHIMONANTHUS PRAECOX* fill the woodland with a sweet perfume at a time of year when we need such treats.

LONICERA FRAGRANTISSIMA has been planted to weave in and out of the hedgerow. Its small, pale, butter-coloured flower is also highly perfumed.

Early-flowering **CROCUS** are planted in the lower pool borders and appear long before the spring perennials. Every year, they reappear in a wave of blue.

HELLEBORUS ORIENTALIS are the backbone of the woodland's lower planting. They have spread throughout the bare patches of soil, filling the woodland with pink and white flowers in profusion in late winter.

The odd early **TULIP** will spot flower only if the winter is mild, their main season being early spring.

SNOWDROPS have been planted under the *Rhododendron* 'Fragrantissimum'. I have started collecting these tiny bulbs in the hope of them naturalising, as they do so easily in England. I am imagining a carpet of pure white flowers in late winter.

All the **EVERGREEN HEDGES** become invaluable in winter. We have hedges of bay, ligustrum and Portuguese laurel. These form the skeleton of the garden and come into their own in winter when all the perennials are cut down. The architecture created by these evergreen hedges is particularly beautiful on a cold misty winter's day.

PREVIOUS PAGE
The pots of tulips love a coating of ice or snow; it makes for a better flowering in the spring.

OPPOSITE The path linking the white garden and the studio.

III

SPRING

During the latter part of winter, I'm always inspecting the box hedging for the swelling buds that will turn it from its wintery bronze to a fresh green. In spite of that, though, spring sneaks up on me when I'm not quite ready for it, as the garden comes alive from its wintery sleep. After enjoying the serenity and calm of winter, the first warmth of spring comes as a great shock. It's never a slow transition from cold to mild but, rather, a couple of jolts of warm days. As glorious as spring is, I know it only means the hot dry weather is not far away. Still, when you get a slight warmth to the day but still have cold nights, it comes a close second to the cold of winter days.

It seems, and I am sure the statistics will prove me correct, that each spring gets drier and the dry weather starts earlier. When I first moved to Stonefields, spring was the wettest of the seasons, whereas now it is just a precursor to the prolonged heat and dry of summer. How I yearn for the days of rain that, almost without fail, we experienced over the two days of our biennial garden weekend in November. Scheduled every second year as a charity event, it managed to pour for four out of five of these weekends. I remember waking up in the morning of the open garden and thinking we must be cursed, as I listened to the torrential rain on the tin roof. Gardeners, resilient souls that they are, however, still came and endured the rain; the sea of umbrellas bobbing around the garden was a sight to be admired. We eventually

PREVIOUS PAGE
A view into the entry courtyard, with a box sphere as its central feature. *Malus spectabilis* trees frame the car forecourt to Stonefields.

OPPOSITE *Wisteria sinensis* shrouds the central marble figure in the rose garden.

moved the event to late autumn to avoid the constant disappointment. I have always maintained that if you want to break a drought, plan an open garden event. That seems to ring true, in that every other year we didn't have the event, it was perfect, dry spring weather.

OPPOSITE Harold the peacock in the entry courtyard. Box and granite spheres are juxtaposed in the simple reflective space.

FOLLOWING PAGE Box spheres create interest in a grouping of pots near the woodland.

STONEFIELDS BY THE SEASONS

DREAMS OF SISSINGHURST

Spring does bring enormous spurts of fresh new growth and flowers to the garden; it starts every year with the electric yellow blossom of the forsythia in the woodland, which is carpeted underneath with flowering hellebores and the rare dogtooth violets. How I love my dogtooth violets – as a young boy I read, with such romantic vision, about Vita Sackville-West growing them at Sissinghurst, and dreamt of the day I could have my own patch. They grow extremely well in our sheltered and well-watered woodland, and I hope that one day they will carpet the sides of the path in huge swathes to complement and subdue the brightness of the forsythia above them. Alas, they are slow to naturalise, and we will be waiting decades to see such a thing.

All the woodland plants are slowly pushing their way above the refuge of their underground hibernation, and many are just as beautiful in bud burst as they are in bloom. In particular, I love the Solomon's seal with its bendy stems all facing in the same direction and rising in unison. I have just started collecting different species and varieties of this woodland plant, some with red stems and others with corkscrew stems. They love our climate and flourish, spreading profusely to the front of the woodland beds that surround the circular central lawn.

Around the woodland, the outer evergreen ring of bay and laurel has now matured and needs cutting back. It has achieved its purpose of providing wind protection, and is now starting to creep towards the centre of the woodland. By removing the inner layer only, we are still protected from the wind, but it has given me more room to plant larger flowering shrubs, such as viburnums

OPPOSITE The marble sculpture is draped with *Wisteria sinensis*.

FOLLOWING PAGE The white garden in early spring. The pleached hornbeam is just coming into leaf, and the beds are full of white tulips.

PAGE 146 *Fritillaria uva-vulpis*.

PAGE 147 *Helleborus orientalis*.

and dogwoods. This part of the garden is also planted with many species and varieties of viburnum, which is one of my favourite large shrubs for shady areas. My absolute favourite remains the commonly used *Viburnum plicatum*; its horizontal branches are smothered in a layer of white flowers in spring. We also have the red-centred *Viburnum sargentii* and *Viburnum opulus*, which has large, white pompom flowers. They are all very tough and require virtually no maintenance, except for the odd cutback every ten years.

I have experimented to find out which variety of dogwood is best for us, and have arrived at *Cornus* 'Constellation'. It seems to be hardier than all the other dogwoods, and flowers reliably in late spring with small but profuse bracts of creamy white. It grows tall and narrow, so fits neatly between the larger oaks and maples.

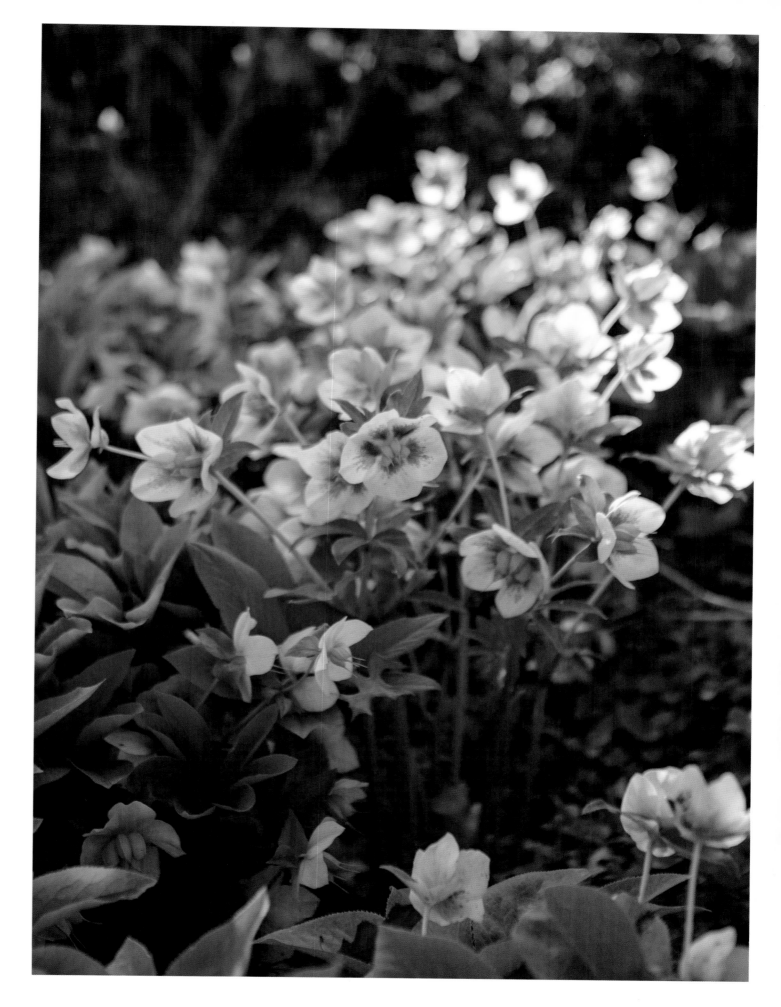

THE APPEAL OF CRAB APPLES

A distinctive sign of early spring at Stonefields is the flowering of the crab apple trees. The main variety is *Malus floribunda*, which present in tight bud as a haze of deep pink, fading to a very pale pink as they fully open. I have planted these small trees in copses of three and five at each corner of the main garden. That number of trees is just enough to create interest, but not too many to become crowded or obscure the main garden from the outer park. The planting also helps soften the sharp corners of the formal hedged layout and allows it to merge into the natural contours of the outer park. In October, the effect is spectacular – the entire park becomes a haze of pink blossom which, if we are lucky, lasts into early November.

Walking around the garden at this time of year, you can really identify certain perfumes, and crab apple is the most recognisable. As there are so many of the trees, and the fragrance is so intoxicating, the entire garden is bathed in it. It's neither sweet nor pungent, but rather distinctive, and is definitely the scent of spring. It's a fragrance I'll never forget, and one that will always be identified in my mind with Stonefields at this time of the year.

Other crab apples I've planted include *Malus sargentii* in the white garden, and *Malus trilobata* in the blue borders, which has a wonderful conical growth habit and spectacular autumn foliage. The *Malus sargentii* blossom is pure white, but only lasts for a few short weeks, after which it falls to the ground like a carpet of confetti. I bought the four *Malus sargentii* specimens, which sit in a cushion of box hedging in each corner of the white garden, as high grafts. They have been grafted onto tall clear stem root

OPPOSITE Blue painted beehives under the *Malus floribunda* trees.

FOLLOWING PAGE *Malus floribunda*.

stock at approximately 1700 millimetres high, thus allowing people to easily walk under them.

I find crab apples are one of the toughest small blossom trees; none of ours receive watering over summer, and they still seem to thrive. Having said that, though, the blue borders each had a *Malus* x *atrosanguinea* 'Gorgeous' in the centre of their beds, but these were a bit hit and miss. If we had a dry spring, they did well, but if we were lucky enough to have a wet one, they were prone to mildew, and this badly affected their flowering. I decided to remove them, and this had the bonus of providing more sun and less competition to the perennials planted beneath. It's always a hard decision to remove trees, especially if you planted them and nurtured them, but I believe it pays to be ruthless in the garden. If there's a great benefit to removing a tree, I don't hesitate.

At the same time as the crab apples, the tulips all come into flower, and the combination is magical. The tulips fill nearly all the rose and perennial beds, as well as the parterre, with the crab apples forming a backdrop. The layering and timing were both considered, and are highly successful. The copper pots I planted in autumn are now crammed full of double layers of tulips exploding from their metallic confines. They sit in front of the herb garden, directly outside the rear door of the house. The collection of old coppers and pots grouped at the door is both welcoming, as this is our main entrance to the house, and a great focal point from the flower room. I only have the one season of flowering in these pots – I find in summer it is too hard to have to water and worry about potted plants in this part of the garden. After the tulips have finished, the coppers are all packed off and stored in the shed.

The parterre is the main show for tulips, starting in late September with the white 'Clearwater' tulips just appearing over the top of the box. In a good season, the entire parterre becomes a sea of white tulip heads. These are closely followed by the slightly higher, deep plum-coloured 'Queen of the Night' tulips; they help extend the flowering time and add another colour to the space. The white garden is also planted with white 'Clearwater' tulips; these don't do too badly, but with competition from the established hornbeams, don't flower as well as those in the parterre. The rose garden looks amazing with its deep red 'Paul Scherer' tulips; these flower when everything else is dormant in this space, and die down just in time for the blanket of anthriscus to cover them later in spring. Every year, we add more tulip bulbs, and every spring, the show gets better and better. They flower at a time when the garden is crying out for colour after a long and muted winter.

OPPOSITE Groupings of old coppers full of tulips provide colour on the herb garden terrace, which is surrounded by a bay hedge.

FOLLOWING PAGE The bell tower in the herb garden, and pots of tulips.

PAGE 156-7 The parterre full of 'Clearwater' tulips filling the negative spaces between the box shapes.

There comes a midpoint in spring, a changing of the guard, when the entire garden is full of crab apple confetti as its frothy blooms fall from the tree and are carried by the ever-present strong spring winds. The tulips are past their prime, and slowly retreat into their bulbs ready for the following year. There's a lull in the flowering, a time before the roses and viburnums, a time when the fresh new growth of the hedges shine, and the perennials cover the entire surface of the soil. It's fleeting, lasting maybe only a week or two, but is enough to make me wonder what plant can fill this void in the flurry of spring flowers. My answer has been alliums; they seem to start flowering just as the tulips finish, and last much longer than them as they tolerate the warmer late spring sun. I have filled the blue borders to the brim with *Allium* 'Purple Rain' and, to date, they have been a great success, naturalising with ease and rewarding us as their heads of blue umbelliferous flowers appear just above the box hedge. I am convinced they will help us counter the effects of global warming as they adapt to the effects of climate change.

OPPOSITE An aerial view of the parterre, apple walk and pool garden.

FOLLOWING PAGE *Allium* 'Purple Rain'.

PAGE 162–3 When the tulips have finished flowering in the blue borders, the beds are filled with *Allium* 'Purple Rain'.

PAGE 164–5 The blue borders full of tulips, before the perennials appear later in spring.

Spring means hedge trimming; the tools we use for the task seem to be going almost constantly at this time of year. The gardeners finish one part of the garden and move straight on to the next. When the entire garden is complete, they start all over again. I adore my hedges, but they are a lot of work.

In the early part of the season, everything is seemingly static, poised ready for the chaos that lies ahead. The buds are swelling and give a fresh tint of green. By mid-spring, the ligustrum hedge is ready for its first trim. We find if we trim it while it is just emerging, this helps maintain its structure. It will go on to be trimmed at least three or four times over the later part of spring and early summer. If I ever left Stonefields and created another garden for myself, I would not plant as many hedges; I'd advise anyone to minimise the amount of hedging they employ. Ligustrum hedges are used here for wind protection and as a kangaroo deterrent, and effectively replace walls in the concept of a walled garden. I have them because I simply couldn't afford walls when I first created the garden. *Ligustrum vulgare* 'Buxifolium' has been a good choice, as it tolerates the heat of summer as well as frost and the occasional dusting of snow in the colder months. I learnt about it after working in the Hamptons on Long Island, New York. This is their main hedging plant, and can be bought at 2 to 3 metres high, which gives instant screening. It's extremely soft, and therefore easy to trim and shape into a variety of forms. The downside is its fast growth habit, which means regular cutting is required. In most parts of Australia, it is banned, so check with your local authority before planting.

The box hedge that defines the inner shape of the garden beds is less labour-intensive as it only needs trimming once a year. The gardeners rigorously debate the timing of this – too early and

FOLLOWING PAGE
The apple walk, with its hedge of *Ligustrum vulgare* 'Buxifolium', early in spring before the apples flower and come into leaf. Spheres of *Buxus sempervirens* are grouped under the apples.

PAGE 170–1 A view through the blue borders, with its ligustrum hedge, and into the white garden.

PAGE 172 *Forsythia* x *intermedia*.

PAGE 173 *Erythronium* 'White Beauty'.

it may need a second trim, but too late and it will burn in the hot sun. We now trim it in late October, or the very first week of November, and hope we don't get a run of hot days. Hot sun on freshly trimmed plants burns them, and they look brown for several months until a fresh layer of growth emerges.

The parterre requires the most time to trim, both because of its need for precision and its massive scale. Every couple of years, I threaten to remove it entirely and replace it with two terraces of flowering perennials. This would look amazing, but I just can't bring myself to discount all the love, sweat and time that has gone into its creation. So, for now it remains and, as labour-intensive as it is, it rewards with its formal precision and form.

We also have three other types of hedges at Stonefields; *Laurus nobilis*, or bay, *Prunus lusitanica*, or Portuguese laurel, and *Cupressus leylandii* 'Leightons Green'. The *Laurus nobilis* that surrounds the herb garden is probably the best hedge in the garden for hardiness, and requires far less trimming than the ligustrum. It requires very little watering either, and has the bonus of producing leaves that can be used in cooking. The *Prunus lusitanica* borders each side of the pool garden, and is an excellent choice for this windy part of the garden. It needs perfect drainage, otherwise it will sit and sulk, and not grow. I enjoy its glossy leaf, and love its leathery feel. The cypress was planted as a windbreak around the vegetable garden and on the eastern side of the service drive – it serves that purpose very well, and we only have to trim it once a year. It is, however, prone to canker, and is only suitable if the soil and water supply is good.

CLOSING THE GAPS

Spring is a time, as well, for patching. Any empty spaces, caused by plants dying or being removed, need to be filled with new plantings. We do this in mid-spring, as it's easy to see what's missing, and there's still time for the new plants to grow and fill the gaps. This is particularly necessary with the perennial plantings, as many of them are short-lived. When I go to Europe, I'm always looking at new perennials, and do much of my research that way for new planting schemes. Sadly, the list of perennials you can choose from in Australia is very limited, compared to what's available overseas; our rightfully strict quarantine laws prevent many from being imported into the country. However, I come back with a list of plants I want to trial at Stonefields, and so find these gaps handy for trying them out. All gardens, and in particular my own, are one big experiment. I think of mine as a laboratory rather than a hospital – if a plant doesn't do well, it's out, and another is trialled.

OPPOSITE Solomon's seal (*Polygonatum* x *hybridum*).

FOLLOWING PAGE 'Clearwater' tulips in the parterre.

Wisteria is one of my favourite climbers. From a very young age, I had command of an overgrown orchard and vegetable garden in a large Edwardian estate next door to the house where I was lucky enough to spend my childhood. The entire property was falling into neglect, and the element I remember most vividly about the orchard was its outer ring of pencil pines covered in wisteria; it was so romantic and wild. At Stonefields, I have used wisteria in unique ways; horizontally as a cushion for my bronze pots on the pool step podiums; vertically on all the masonry pillars marking the entrance to each garden and, more commonly, over the pergola to the lilac walk. The most inventive and beautiful use is as a shroud to the sculpture in the rose garden. This was once a marble statue of Jesus that I bought from a wrecking yard when I was a teenager. My parents were horrified to see Jesus arrive in their garden, but I saw, minus his head and arms, he would become a Roman antiquity – something I had always coveted, but could never afford. He since followed me to my house in Prahran, St Ambrose Farm and now Stonefields. He looked far too large for the rose garden, so I decided the best way to reduce him in scale, and also integrate him into the garden, was by shrouding him in wisteria. A metal frame in the shape of a small tree was made to train it over, so every spring, he has been wrapped in a cloth of sweet-smelling wisteria. This perfume transports me straight back to those carefree days spent slashing unruly grass under ancient, non-productive fruit trees. As you will read in the summer chapter, the statue has now been taken away from the rose garden and hence so has the wisteria. It was very hard to remove this very established and reliable flowering plant, but good design always comes first, and the rose garden looks all the better for his absence.

OPPOSITE The wisteria-draped marble statue.

FOLLOWING PAGE *Wisteria sinensis.*

PAGE 182-3 An aerial view into the rose garden, blue borders, white garden, apple walk and parterre.

PAGE 184 *Clematis armandii* 'Apple Blossom'.

PAGE 185 *Fritillaria meleagris.*

APPLE AND LILAC WALKS

The apple walk is particularly beautiful in the spring with the 'Crimson Crisp' apples flowering at the same time as the box clouds are flush with their new growth and wisteria covers the twin pavilion façades. Rarely do all components of a single part of the garden peak together, but here they do.

Productivity in the garden was high on our wish list, hence the choice of fruiting apples, which also form a protective canopy to the serpentine bed of large box spheres at their feet. They always crop in a two-year cycle, with one year giving us a very small crop or none at all, and the next guaranteed to be a bumper harvest. The linear nature of the walk, combined with its central position, was designed to give articulation to the square form of the parterres and blue borders. To soften the interface between the two very formal gardens, we chose to create the serpentine bed. The apples and clouds of box also help as a softening agent between these two very formal gardens.

The newly created lilac walk was designed to be an end point of the garden, and a link between the house field and woodland. According to all our growers and suppliers, lilacs are out of fashion, so getting hold of that quantity was nearly impossible. Luckily, we found one grower who had two varieties, 'Congo' and 'Charles Joly'. We bought all the plants he had, and they now line the walk that starts at the woodland steps and terminates at a wisteria pergola leading into the home field. They have proven to be extremely easy to look after and to get to flower. In spring the plants come alive with huge bunches of grape-like mauve flowers that have an amazing perfume. I have underplanted them with

OPPOSITE The apple walk with the 'Crimson Crisp' apples in flower.

FOLLOWING PAGE Harold in the rose garden. The photo was taken after the statue had been removed and the loose pebbles replaced with granite paving.

species geraniums, *Persicaria affinis* and *Ceratostigma willmottianum*. Like many plants in the garden, the lilac was chosen for picking as cut flowers for the house. There is nothing better than abundance, and being able to go out and pick armfuls of lilac flowers for the house is my idea of extravagance. They last for weeks if cut just before fully opening and if you also split the bottom of the stems before plunging them into a deep vase of water.

The perennial beds of the pool garden, lower pool beds and blue borders are not in full bloom during spring, but are certainly warming up for their main show of summer and autumn. The *Salvia nemorosa* of the lower twin beds and the agastache of the blue borders start flowering and don't stop until mid-autumn. All the foliage of the other plants fill the entire beds, overtaking the remnants of the bulbs.

MEMORIES OF MARNANIE

One often under-visited part of the garden is the small path, running beside the pool fence, that connects the side of the house to the kookaburra gate. It has a sloping bed to one side, planted with *Anemone* x *hybrida*, *Hydrangea paniculata* and *Rhododendron* 'Fragrantissimum'. This rhododendron is one of my all-time favourite plants; it reminds me of my days at Marnanie at Mt Macedon in Victoria where, when I was young, I worked in the garden with the late Kevin O'Neill. Kevin was, without doubt, the best florist Australia has ever seen, and his garden was a place of abundance, supplying his shop with masses of unusual and interesting flowers. In one part, there was a pond fed by a natural spring – the path beside it was lined with *Hydrangea paniculata* and *Rhododendron* 'Fragrantissimum', which flowered in the spring. I so distinctly remember the florist shop, and this part of the garden being filled with the sweet cinnamon smell of the rhododendron. I was desperate to be reminded of that, so planted the entire bank with it. In spring we are able to pick armfuls of flowers to bring inside and let it fill the house with its sweet scent. In summer, the *Hydrangea paniculata* comes into flower, but sadly cannot be picked as it flops after a few hours.

The warmer days and cool nights of late spring are particularly appealing – the coolness and dew keep the fields green, and the warmth during the day helps growth in the beds. The garden is full again after its patchy start to the season; the perennials are beginning to show hints of flowers; the roses are just starting to bloom, and the woodland is full of the scented dogwood and viburnum blossom. It's the peak time for the garden, with most

OPPOSITE The pavilion I designed in 1987 for the late Kevin O'Neill at Mt Macedon.

plants in flower and the house field hopefully still green, so we open it to the public to raise funds for charity. We often get more than 9000 visitors in a single weekend. It's rewarding to see so many people enjoying it, but at the same time worrying about the damage that can be done to the lawns. For the most part, the garden copes well, and in fact, far better than I expect.

HEDGE TRIMMING is the most time-consuming activity, involving all the large hedges of ligustrum, prunus, laurus and cypress as well as the lower layer of box hedging. We use petrol-powered cutters for the larger hedges of ligustrum, prunus and cypress and very sharp hand shears for the more delicate box hedges and spheres. It's very important to get the weather onside when pruning the box; we have to hope there are no days of more than 25 degrees Celsius for at least a week afterwards, as hot sun will burn the more delicate foliage exposed during clipping. To avoid bruising and ripping the leaves, we make sure the tools are very sharp. It's also critical to use a string line to make sure the hedge is cut perfectly straight.

At this time of year, the main **LAWNS ARE MOWN** often twice a week, with the house field mown weekly.

All the perennials and roses need **STAKING** as they grow during spring; this prevents them from falling over under the weight of their flowers. We grow hazel bushes for the sole purpose of cutting the branches for staking; they are suitably gnarly and strong enough to support the perennials. For the more robust plants, we have made steel rings welded to steel rods, which are placed over the perennials in winter to allow them to grow through the ring for support.

In preparation for spring, we do a lot of our feeding of **COMPOST** and slow-release **GRANULAR FERTILISERS** during winter, but we are always topping this up in spring when the growth is rapid and requires a lot of nutrition.

OPPOSITE 'Clearwater' tulips in the parterre.

ROSES are in full bloom in later spring. 'Gertrude Jekyll', with its full cabbage-shaped and deeply perfumed flowers, is the main burgundy rose in the rose garden. 'Wedding Day', a very large and vigorous climbing rose, is planted over the potting shed, and has showers of white flowers. 'Pierre de Ronsard', which grows up the walls of the rose garden, is the most reliable and prolific pink flowering climbing rose. 'Crépuscule' and 'Mermaid' cover the roof of the twin pool pavilions; they start flowering in spring and continue until the end of summer.

AGASTACHE 'SWEET LILI' is planted in the blue borders. Its hot pink flowers intensify the blue of the other perennials around it.

AGASTACHE 'BLUE BOA' is the best of the blue-flowering agastaches. It is more compact than its similar cousin 'Blue Fortune', and its intense blue flowers last all spring and summer, and well into the autumn.

SALVIA NEMOROSA is the low-growing blue salvia that forms the bulk of the lower pool flower borders. It will flush with flowers three times over the spring and summer period if it is cut back after each flowering.

With its grey foliage and cream flowers, *ANTHEMIS* 'SUSANNAH MITCHELL', a large groundcover, is planted in the pool borders and fills in the corners of the beds. It's prolific in its flowering, and will benefit from being cut back regularly over the spring.

We have many summer-flowering **CLEMATIS**. The main ones are in the rose garden and climb up through the wisterias on each pillar beside the gates. We cut these plants to the ground each winter and allow them to grow throughout the summer without any further pruning.

I have always used **WISTERIA** to either cover walls of houses or architectural features. At Stonefields, it is used to create cradles of foliage and flowers for the pots on the rear terrace. It covers the verandah and pergolas of the farmhouse. It is very reliable and drought hardy, and will also spot flower over summer, extending its flowering season.

Planted by the thousands in autumn, **TULIPS** are the mainstay of our spring bulb season. I use them in pots and coppers on the side terrace, as well as in the rose garden and parterres. We are able to leave them in the ground at Stonefields and they will successfully come back and flower year after year.

We plant thousands of **BLUEBELLS** each year in the woodland and lilac walk. They flower reliably, creating a carpet of blue in early spring. They naturalise very easily and require little to no maintenance.

The small and delicate **FRITILLARIAS** are restricted to pots. These flowering bulbs are irresistible to rabbits, and will quickly disappear if planted in garden beds.

DAFFODILS are not my favourite bulb, but we inherited them in the garden of the farmhouse from the previous owners, and have since planted many more each side of the drive to the farmhouse. At last count, there were 4000.

ALLIUMS are rapidly becoming my favourite bulb. Related to garlic, they are hardier than tulips, and do extremely well in the blue borders. They flower longer than a tulip and naturalise easily. The flower also lasts for up to six weeks.

SOLOMON'S SEAL is planted in the front of the woodland garden beds. This unusual herbaceous perennial flowers with tiny green bells along the length of the stem. Great for picking for the house.

HOSTAS are often hard to grow in Australia, but they love our cooler mountain air. They thrive in the woodland and I have planted them mostly for their large, lush sculptural leaves.

I have used only white **ASTILBE** as I find the pink varieties too garish. They love the shade and cool of our woodland.

I have experimented with a few dogwoods and found the variety **CORNUS 'CONSTELLATION'** to be the best for our conditions. Flowering in mid-spring, it is great for picking and bringing inside to fill a large vase.

VIBURNUM OPULUS, which is planted in the woodland, has white spheres of flowers and is great for picking.

VIBURNUM PLICATUM, which is also in the woodland, has delicate white blooms appearing along the length of its branches.

I have planted two clumps of the white feathery flowered perennial, **ARUNCUS**, on either side of the woodland path.

EUPHORBIA ROBBIAE thrives in the woodland as it grows up to the trunks of the oak trees. Its acid green flowers are electric in the shade of the tree canopies.

RHODODENDRON 'FRAGRANTISSIMUM' is a small and highly perfumed rhododendron planted en masse in the lower woodland path. It's not beautiful, with its form being woody and not lush, but it's worth it for the flowers and sweet scent.

ANTHRISCUS SYLVESTRIS is a burgundy foliage plant that grows under the rose bushes, complementing the red-flowered blooms. In spring it erupts into sprays of white flowers.

I have inherited a black unnamed **FLAG IRIS** from a dear friend and it now lives in our rose garden.

AQUILEGIA VULGARIS 'RUBY PORT' is the crimson variety that flowers in the rose garden. It's delicate enough in form to grow between the roses without smothering them.

MALUS FLORIBUNDA is our main crab apple, and looks spectacular when it's flowering at this time of year.

LONICERA PERICLYMENUM is a honeysuckle that requires no watering, but rewards us with masses of fragrant deep pink blooms.

MOLLIS AZALEAS are slightly scented. We have these in pots and bring them into the house when they flower in spring.

SYRINGA VULGARIS, or lilac, appears in our newly created lilac walk. My main variety is 'Congo', and it has masses of grape-like deep mauve and highly perfumed flowers.

IV

SUMMER

Summer is heralded by the arrival of the black cockatoos. They appear like clockwork in the sky, usually in pairs or small flocks, in search of ripe pine cones to feast on. Their call is one of the sounds that dominate the garden during the warmer months, along with the constant hum of the cicadas high in the trees and the disruptive sound of the hedge trimmers trying to keep up with the summer growth.

It's the most challenging time of year as, because of the heat, we are always monitoring the wellbeing of the garden. Rain comes rarely, but if it does, it's light and doesn't last – the garden totally relies on irrigation to nurture it through the season. We do everything we can to help minimise the need for supplementary watering, mulching heavily using our own compost, selecting plants that have low water requirements, and protecting the garden from the hot dry northerly winds.

Summer is the season for retreating to the cool inner core of the house during the day, and venturing out in the early evening and mornings or, occasionally, for a swim in the hot midday sun. These are not the months for me to garden, but instead to plan and design for the garden.

PREVIOUS PAGE
Summer in the rose garden, as the dahlias are just starting to flower.

OPPOSITE
The woodland becomes a green haven in summer; with protection from hot winds, it's cooler than surrounding parts of the garden.

FOLLOWING PAGE
The blue borders, with *Agastache* 'Blue Fortune' and *Eutrochium maculatum* 'Gateway' in bud.

THE CONCEPT OF PARADISE

As it matures, the garden becomes more and more protected. The windbreaks I planted fifteen years ago now provide an enormous amount of protection, and the hedges are all tall enough to shelter the more delicate areas closer to the house. When the house was first built, the hedges were only 30 centimetres high, and the wind made a very scary noise as it howled around the building. It made me wonder why I had built in such an exposed location. Now that the hedges and trees are at their mature height, I hardly hear the wind inside the house, and only faintly in the adjacent garden areas. It's amazing how, if designed correctly, a garden can protect you and your home.

The ancient, and still relevant, notion of a garden being paradise was all about an environment that was a respite from the harsh surrounding desert, a place full of water, with walls sheltering the space from hot wind, and trees providing shade. I still create gardens following this centuries-old tradition. It's particularly necessary at Stonefields, because of our exposure to the hot northerly winds formed from Australia's inland deserts, and the cold southwesterly winter winds straight from Antarctica. We are helped slightly due to our elevation, which provides us with cooler temperatures, but we are still what I consider a hostile environment in summer for plants and humans. The concept of a walled garden, with hedges rather than brick or stone for walls, has paid off enormously, as most garden rooms are now totally protected from the wind.

The other vital ingredient in those gardens of paradise was the use of water, which was often transported vast distances

under the hot desert sands in man-made channels to appear above ground in rills and fountains. The result was both physically and emotionally cooling to anyone using the garden on a hot summer's day. I have re-created this at Stonefields in the form of the main rill that runs from the top of the garden, with its spurting bronze snake emerging out of the ligustrum hedge and separating the entry courtyard from the blue borders. The rill then forms the main spine of the garden, passing down the centre of each staircase that intersects the front garden terraces. In summer, I can't wait to turn it on in the morning. Just seeing each snake fountain, with its vertical jet of water, makes the heat seem more bearable.

FIRE GUARD

A huge challenge in summer is bushfires; Central Victoria is one of the most bushfire-prone areas in the world. I have put in place significant fire retardation measures to help mitigate their threat. These include buffers of European deciduous trees; keeping the paddock grass low; and creating green zones, made up of lush foliage full of water and resistant to burning, between the house and the probable path of any potential fires. We are a good distance from the bushland, which works in our favour, but are located on top of the hill, which works against us. Fire races at incredible speeds and force up hills. We have had a number of fires near us, and have spent many panic-stricken days watching smoke and distant flames approach, only to be extinguished by our highly talented volunteer firefighters.

My very geographically targeted app to notify me of local fires seems to send me alerts every day, which is yet more reason why I find summer difficult. That said, there are, of course, many reasons to love it. It's the time of the year when the garden is full of flowers; the rose garden and all the perennial gardens are in full bloom and loving the heat and dry of summer. Unlike a lot of the east coast of Australia, we are not subject to high humidity, which is the enemy of many plants. We have, in fact, honed our planting scheme to things that enjoy the heat and dry. Roses, herbaceous perennials, bay and laurel hedges, and oak trees all endure our dry heat extremely well.

OPPOSITE *Agastache* 'Blue Boa'.

FOLLOWING PAGE
A view along the apple walk, from the pavilion to the central snake fountain.

INSPIRED BY THE ROSE GARDENS OF SHIRAZ

The rose garden was formerly the vegetable garden, and was created when I hedged two sides and built a high rendered wall to the other two sides. It was designed as four large beds to facilitate the necessary rotation of annual vegetable plantings. After two years of ebbing and flowing in and out of love with the messy, unpredictable and ever-changing nature of vegetable gardens, I decided it needed to be banished to the working part of the property, near the large gardener's shed. Here it could flourish at certain times of the year, and look messy at others, without being seen in the main decorative part of the garden. But then I had to work out what to do with its former location. The solution came to me when I was in Iran on a garden and archaeological tour, and, in particular, when I saw the many beautiful rose gardens of Shiraz. These are very different from the English-style rose gardens we are used to. Rather than being full of frothy pale roses underplanted with masses of cottage plants, they are, in fact, more masculine in feel, with hotter and often clashing colours.

Given my garden is very controlled in its form, a pretty pale pink rose garden had never seemed right, whereas I was excited by the deep red, maroon and plum colours of Shiraz. I wanted the entire garden to feel like a Persian rug, with its complexity of deep colours and fullness of texture. The main rose I initially chose was 'William Shakespeare', a deep red and highly fragrant David Austin variety. It was the perfect colour, fragrance and form, being a full cabbage rose, and had a wonderfully healthy spring flush.

However, during summer, it developed a persistent fungal disease, which caused the flowers to ball. For some years, I persevered, but have now replaced it with 'Munstead Wood', another David Austin variety but less prone to fungal diseases.

The underplanting was probably more important than the rose choice, as the plants had to be good companions to roses and complement their colour scheme. The two main perennials I chose were *Anthriscus sylvestris* and a deep plum *Aquilegia vulgaris*. The anthriscus, or raven's wing, has deep mauve foliage and, in spring, fills the voids between the roses with sprays of white umbelliferous flowers. Although the main flush of the rose garden is in late spring, it's very much a summer garden and one from which I can reliably cut flowers for the house. There's nothing better than a huge vase of roses freshly cut from the garden – every week during summer, I manage to get a sizeable bunch.

A MORE RELAXED ATTITUDE

At the time of writing, the garden is nearly fifteen years old and, with the exception of the major trees such as oaks and sequoias, feeling fairly mature. All the hedges are at their required height, the garden beds are full and flourishing, and the house is settled into its landscape with the help of its cloak of vines. As I've mentioned, with this maturity comes both a sense of joy and dilemma. I love creating new spaces and seeing major change but, as Stonefields approaches its desired form and maturity, there's not much need for change. However, one thing that has altered is my more relaxed style towards garden design. This evolving sense of casualness, in allowing the plants the freedom to just be and fall where they wish, is at odds with some areas of my own garden. I no longer want to contain the plants within borders of box hedging, but prefer they fall over the edge of paths, lawns and paving, and occupy gaps in the paving or gravel.

The rose garden has been a perfect starting point for this transition in the garden's direction. It was a very hard decision, but the first victim was the marble statue of Jesus I have owned since childhood, and moved from house to house. From the very inception of the garden, though, I was worried that he did not match the scale of the double snake fountain in the blue borders. As you looked through the blue borders into the rose garden from the white garden, he and the fountain were in a direct axis. His size and placement also blocked the view through the far gates out to the paddocks beyond. The decision was made to remove him and, at the same time, remove part of the cypress hedge beyond to allow an oak tree to be our distant focal point. That

OPPOSITE The two Chinese elms (*Ulmus parvifolia*) planted into the table will eventually act as living umbrellas, providing shade in summer.

FOLLOWING PAGE A view of the front garden from the upstairs bedroom window. In summer there are lots of flowers in the borders, and the box hedge is an intense green.

SUMMER

made a difference immediately; the line of sight was elongated, the garden felt less cluttered and the snake sculpture's scale was restored. I felt the shackles of European ornamentation had been removed.

The next major change to the rose garden was the removal of the large grey pebbles covering the path. These were laboriously replaced with shards of irregular lengths of Italian granite. The texture and imperfection of this stone excites me, along with the ability to allow for pockets of groundcovers. It's difficult to lay the stone, due to its thickness and variation in size, but this provides the aged character I like so much. The gardeners, who are always overloaded with tasks, insisted on laying it. That's because, like most people in their line of work, they don't like outsiders invading their territory, and are highly critical of any other trade that tries to do so. The stone had to fit together like a jigsaw puzzle, with varying sizes dovetailing into each other, which was a laborious, time-consuming task. I prefer the finished effect to look as if it has been there for 200 years, but unfortunately, I never win this type of battle, as the gardeners seek perfection every time.

We're constantly at loggerheads over this. I have visited, and desired, too many ancient European gardens to want everything to look immaculate and perfect. I would prefer the paving to appear as if a tree root deep underground had caused it to be raised slightly in places.

Despite this, the reworked rose garden is a great improvement. The paths are easier to walk on and have far more character than the pebbles; the selection of roses has finally been refined to display vigour and the preferred colour; and the removal of the statue has opened up the vista and created a huge sense of space. The beds will always need tweaking, but so does every garden bed. This is what gardening is all about – you can never rest and think a planting scheme will remain as it is.

OPPOSITE A detail of the parterre.

PAGE 224 *Aster* x *frikartii* 'Mönch', with *Agastache* 'Blue Boa' and *Agastache* 'Sweet Lili' in the background.

PAGE 225 *Eutrochium maculatum* 'Gateway'.

OPENING UP THE HERB GARDEN

The next part of the garden to have its box hedge removed was the herb garden. This is a very much a spring and summer garden – spring when all the tulips are out, and summer when it is full of herbs and the occasional splash of flowering perennials. The garden used to consist of compartments delineated by box hedges, with a separate space for each herb type. As time went by, the hedges got thicker, meaning the space for each herb became smaller, and my desire for more softness and freedom increased. The only solution was to remove the hedges, which again met huge resistance from the gardeners. Finally, a compromise was reached, in which the internal hedges creating the compartments would be removed, and the external border kept. The result was instant liberation. The garden felt larger, and the massing of herbs and perennials also looked far more substantial, thus providing greater impact.

Due to its proximity to the back door, this is a very important part of the garden, as we see it every time we go in and out of the house. It's also on our well-worn route to the vegetable garden, and is so well visited that I commissioned Beau Johnstone to make me a faux bois bench for it. Beau is one of my great recent discoveries – we met on Instagram after I posted a photo of my old French faux bois bench in the woodland. After making contact, I discovered she had gone to America to learn the rare craft of making fake timber furniture out of concrete, which was first done by the French in the eighteenth century. It has recently come back into fashion – its rustic character suits country gardens, and it has the benefit of never needing to be painted or protected.

The addition of the new bench allows us to sit in this very protected part of the garden and have a cup of tea on a sunny winter's day. To do this, though, the herb garden really needed to look good all year round. So, after removing the internal box hedging and paving the space with the same granite blocks as the rose garden, the beds were replanted with a mixture of herbs, euphorbia, wallflowers, foxgloves and iris. The garden, these days, is far more interesting and beautiful than it used to be.

THE EARLY MORNING WALK

On hot summer days, you can usually find us in one of two places — either inside seeking shade and relief from the heat or dining and entertaining on the rear vine-covered terrace. Either way, we usually start the day with a very early morning walk with Ruby before it gets hot. It follows a well-rehearsed routine, as she races through the front door and makes for the top of the stairs in the blue borders. She stops here to look back and make sure we're not far behind. We leave the main garden via the white garden, and then decide whether we should walk around the gravel path bordering the lawn or cut straight across the lawn, as most people do. Usually the shorter distance wins. From there, it's out through the blue gates and into the house paddock, where Ruby runs around playing cat and mouse with her very willing playmates, the magpies. It's here that I stop and admire the oak trees I planted some fifteen years ago. They are far from mature, but still convey the message of promise and hope that one day we will be driving under them, sheltering from the hot sun. These oak trees, and hundreds of others that I have planted around the property, keep me tied to this piece of land that contained only a few ancient and very precious manna gums when I first arrived here. There is something very special about the oaks — now they have enough height to walk under, they seem to capture you and hold on to you until you just cannot leave them.

After the obligatory pause at the oaks, we pass through the gatehouse arch and into the front paddock, which is the juncture between us and the outside world. Cattle used to graze here under a few well-protected trees, which kept the grass under control. Every year, though, I planted more oaks; eventually there were so many

OPPOSITE The blue borders in full summer flower.

of them that we could not produce enough elaborate wooden tree guards, so I banished the cattle to the bottom paddock. This had two benefits — firstly, because the grass could grow longer, I could mow wide paths into it. I love the contrast between long and mown grass — it reminds me of walking through an English wildflower meadow. Secondly, in the absence of heavy and destructive cattle hooves, I could repair the leaking lake and keep it full all summer, instead of relying on constant winter inflow of rain and its runoff.

No cattle also meant there were no limits on the planting of trees. The paddock — now more grandly known as the park — is full of oaks and a few umbrella pines. One of my first plantings fifteen years ago was a wide strip of pin oaks. They sat and sulked for many years, requiring more water than I was willing to give them. I have learnt my lesson and, in the interests of greater sustainability, I now plant Algerian oaks, which require virtually no water and flourish on neglect. They can also be evergreen — a big plus with our fashion for deciduous trees at Stonefields.

Our walk can vary through this part of the property; some days it's via the mown paths, and on others, it's along the gravel drive, past the enormous compost heaps, and back home. If it's not too hot, we follow the same route early in the evening, once the sun has retreated behind Kangaroo Hill, to our west.

OPPOSITE When the grass dries off in summer in the paddock, it takes on the appearance of hay.

FOLLOWING PAGE The ligustrum hedge separates the car park from the house paddock, which is planted with *Malus floribunda*.

PAGE 236–7 The studio, with Boston ivy (*Parthenocissus tricuspidata*) on the wall and *Wisteria sinensis* trained along the fascia.

THE JOY OF CATALOGUES

On summer days when I'm sheltering inside from the heat, it's the perfect time for planning the autumn bulb and perennial planting. This involves poring over a multitude of catalogues, as well as cross-checking what plants did, and did not, perform well the previous year. The bulbs are my favourite, and I can spend many hours dreaming of how the coppers will look in spring, and what new fritillarias I can plant in the woodland. The catalogues are a terrible source of temptation – it's hard not to over-order as there are so many beautiful colours and new varieties to choose from. We are blessed at Stonefields to have the best bulb grower in Australia support us with our plantings. Tesselaar has been around for decades, and they kindly give me hundreds of tulips and daffodils to try in the garden each year. Through their generosity, which I'm extremely grateful for, gardeners can see how bulbs can be used on a very large scale, so hopefully Tesselaar receives some benefit, too.

OPPOSITE Tulips in the old coppers.

FOLLOWING PAGE The apple walk in fruit.

PAGE 242 The rear façade of the house is shaded by the *Vitis coignetiae* vine.

PAGE 243 *Clematis* 'Golden Tiara'.

EVOLUTION OF
THE TERRACE

OPPOSITE The view
from the rear terrace
to the pool garden, with
its summer display of
flowering perennials.
Sanguisorba 'Cangshan
Cranberry' and *Thalictrum
flavum* can be seen in
the foreground.

FOLLOWING PAGE
A low hedge of *Cotoneaster
horizontalis* lies between
the pool lounges and the
garden bed.

PAGE 248-9
The lower twin pool
borders, looking out to
the valley below, feature
Penstemon 'Firebird',
Geranium 'Rozanne'
and *Salvia nemorosa*.

In the heat of summer, one part of the garden that always stays cool, and is therefore used as much as possible, is the terrace off the kitchen. It has a pergola covered in *Vitis coignetiae*, which not only provides shelter to the 5-metre dining table, which seats twenty, but also shades the kitchen from the sun. We have recently added the same pergola to the terrace off the main bedroom, making an enormous difference to the heat load of the room.

The only room we can't stop the sun from reaching is the main living room. It's the central core of the building, faces north, and protrudes more than a metre further out than the kitchen and bedroom wings. To add a pergola here would take away the three-dimensionality of the building, as it would run the length of the house. The only solution was to grow the vitis on a wire against the building, and allow it to droop down over the windows in summer.

Over the years, the vine above the table has been trained over the top to block the midday sun, and down the sides enough to prevent the setting sun from reaching the table, but not too far to obstruct our view of the garden and valley below.

When we're using the table for a special function, there's always the risk of rain. Every time it threatens to, I swear one day I will build a pavilion, with a solid roof and walls, to protect us from flies and wasps. The terrace, though, has the benefit of being elevated, and close to the pool perennial borders, giving the impression of floating in a sea of flowering plants. They reach their peak in summer, timed especially for those outdoor entertaining occasions. Thalictrum, achillea, calamagrostis and sanguisorba were chosen as their flowering height is at the level of the terrace.

The vegetable garden flourishes in the summer months as long as it is kept well watered. We can sustain ourselves entirely from its produce, and make a rule never to buy any fruit or vegetables during this period, instead letting the garden dictate what we cook and eat. It is a time for fast growth; lettuces can be harvested in six weeks, and the smaller micro-salads we sow as seed can be picked in three weeks. This style of summer greens is now our favourite; using rocket, beetroot, radish, small lettuces and the like, we plant them very densely, allowing 200 millimetres between rows. We can harvest them as soon as the foliage is at a height suitable for salads; cutting them to the ground, they soon reappear and can be re-cut many times over.

Our garlic, planted at Easter and harvested at Christmas, is picked and stored on racks in the old potting shed in the rose garden. When the rose garden was the vegetable garden, this building was the chicken house, and has made a very successful transition into a potting shed. Buried deep under a bower of 'Wedding Day' rose and wisteria, it remains a cool airy space, perfect for storing our excess vegetables. Other regular and reliable summer produce include zucchini (always in abundance), cucumbers, carrots, beans, peas and tomatoes.

Over the past few years, we have started training our berries on metal and timber frames, which keeps them narrow and easy to harvest. Gooseberries, raspberries, blackberries and loganberries are all grown this way. I look forward to the daily trip from the house down the hill to the vegetable garden, which usually happens in both the morning and evening. Ruby seeks out the many rabbits we share our produce with, while we sit on the bench in the shade at the end of the garden. We discuss what we

OPPOSITE Rainbow chard and dill in the vegetable garden.

PAGE 252 Broccoli and kale under a willow frame.

PAGE 253 Strawberries grow under the gooseberries. Summer vegetables can be seen in the background.

PAGE 254–5 The sheltered woodland has its own microclimate, offering respite from the wind and heat in summer.

would like to grow, and what is, and isn't, doing well. As with other sections of the garden, if a plant doesn't do well, we don't persist with its cultivation. Our biggest failure in the vegetable garden has been strawberries. No matter what we do, we get no fruit. The solution would be simply not to grow them; every winter we plan to get rid of them, but they're still there.

As the end of summer approaches, the seasonal flowers progressively fade; many of the perennials would expire if we didn't repeatedly cut them back to encourage more flowering. As the heat and dry persist, I look forward to the cooling of autumn and its explosion of colour in our trees.

This is the time of year for **STAKING AND DEAD-HEADING** of perennials. Many, such as the *Salvia nemorosa* and *Geranium* 'Rozanne', will have up to three flushes of flowers if they are cut back hard by approximately two-thirds.

To **PROMOTE FLOWERING,** we constantly cut all dead flower heads off roses as this brings on more blooms.

TOUGHER HEDGES, such as the ligustrum and prunus, are trimmed to maintain their shape and form. Softer ones, such as the box, however, will burn if cut back in summer, so we leave this until the cooler months of autumn.

Ensuring the newly planted trees don't dry out takes up much of the gardeners' time in summer. This requires a good **WEEKLY WATERING** using the water tank, and the trees are heavily mulched each year to help prevent evaporation. All our pots are now on irrigation, which has saved a huge amount of time, as previously they needed to be watered every day.

LAWNS need constant attention as this is their main growing season. They are cut every week, and properly watered and fed. The outer fields receive no water. They die off in summer, but always green up in the late autumn.

It's the time of year for **TIP PRUNING,** which involves reducing the ends of long runners of growth on climbers such as wisteria and ornamental grape. Regular tip pruning of summer growth, instead of one heavy prune in winter, helps maintain flowering spurs on wisteria.

WEEDING is a major task in summer. We try to minimise weed growth by mulching heavily and achieving dense plant coverage to each bed. Despite our best efforts, weeds still grow.

The **BOSTON IVY** on the house grows like mad in summer, and needs a weekly trim around the window and door frames. It's a lot of work, but to see the house covered and softened by its glossy green foliage is worth all the trouble.

OPPOSITE
Hydrangea paniculata.

WISTERIA, one of my favourite climbers and one that I've used in various places in the garden, has a summer flush of misty flowers.

HERBACEOUS PERENNIALS love the heat and dry, and we only use plants that flower all summer, such as salvia, agastache, achillea, nepeta, geranium, penstemon, anthemis and caryopteris.

If we contintue to cut the **SALVIA NEMOROSA** back, it will repeat flower over summer.

The same goes for **NEPETA 'DROPMORE'**, which will flower again in summer if cut back after its spring flush.

The main agastaches are **AGASTACHE 'SWEET LILI'**, **AGASTACHE 'BLUE BOA'** and **AGASTACHE 'BLUE FORTUNE'**.

Our achillea is **ACHILLEA 'ANTIQUE PARCHMENT'**.

We find **GERANIUM 'ROZANNE'** is the best flowering geranium for Stonefields – its mid-blue flowers flush from late spring to early autumn.

PENSTEMON 'FIREBIRD' has red flowers that bloom all summer.

CALAMAGROSTIS x ACUTIFLORA 'KARL FOERSTER' is the best flowering ornamental grass for our area. Its tall hay-coloured flowers are the main accents in the pool borders.

'GERTRUDE JEKYLL' ROSE flowers all summer, as does our climbing **'PIERRE DE RONSARD'** in both red and pink.

All the rugosa roses flower over the summer months; **ROSA RUGOSA 'ALBA'** with its single-petal white blooms, **ROSA RUGOSA 'RUGSPIN'** spot flowers all summer with its lilac pink flowers.

'ROSERAIE DE L'HAY' is the rugosa rose in the rose garden. Its deep maroon flowers complement the red of the neighbouring 'Gertrude Jekyll'.

HYDRANGEA QUERCIFOLIA, with its grape-shaped white flowers, will tolerate some sun and does well in our woodland path, which receives morning sun.

HYDRANGEA PANICULATA will tolerate full sun and grows to become a medium-sized bush.

HYDRANGEA MACROPHYLLA needs total shade, and does well under the hornbeams in the white garden.

PERSICARIA AFFINIS and **CERATOSTIGMA WILLMOTTIANUM** start flowering in late summer and continue well into the autumn. They extend the flowering season of the lilac walk, which is spectacular in spring when the lilac is in bloom.

OPPOSITE *Agastache* 'Blue Boa' and *Agastache* 'Sweet Lili'.

FOLIAGE SHRUBS include smoke bush, cherry laurel and maples.

AGAPANTHUS CAMPANULATUS 'ISIS', with its slender, delicate blue flower heads, appears late summer in the blue borders.

GALTONIA CANDICANS is a summer bulb that has tall spikes of pure white flowers that sit proudly above the blue perennials.

VERONICASTRUM VIRGINICUM is a white flowering herbaceous perennial that grows in the white garden, flourishing despite the competition from the roots of the hornbeam trees.

SANGUISORBA 'CANGSHAN CRANBERRY' is a red-flowered herbaceous perennial, planted in the pool flower borders. It has small tufts of flowers appearing on long narrow branches.

CONCLUSION

This spring, as I walk around Stonefields, I experienced the feeling that any creator seeks – that of satisfaction and wellbeing. It's almost a full stop at the end of a very long gardening sentence. It's the first season I have actually felt this euphoric sense of achievement in the garden rather than being focused on the missing ingredients or mistakes. I can, at last, relax and enjoy the fruits of my physical and creative input. Oak trees I planted fifteen years ago now provide scale and mass to the garden; the hedges that form the rooms to the main garden are dense and at their desired height, providing the much-needed architectural form; and the garden beds that sit at their feet are brimming full of floriferous plant material. There is always room for change in the garden beds, but basically the plants all suit the climatic conditions, including the newly shaded areas of the garden that started out life in full sun.

My only challenge here is now to adapt to a rapidly changing climate, which in my view is entirely man-made. The summers are definitely becoming longer and hotter, and so we must adapt to this with our planting choices. On my travels to hot dry countries, such as Greece, Italy and parts of the Middle East, I am constantly searching for plants that do well in prolonged, hot, dry summers. They are often native to these countries, found along the roadside or on long morning walks before the heat of the day. I've discovered many such plants, including phlomis, different types of rosemary, salvia and thyme, and integrated them into the garden at Stonefields.

A tragic additional impact of climate change is the increased fire risk, which is totally out of our control. All we can do is prepare the house and garden as best we can by creating green spaces near the house, keeping the paddock grass short and equipping the house with fire hoses and pumps.

After being supplemented with our own compost for fifteen years, our soil is now rich in organic material, complementing the already well-drained volcanic soil we inherited. As long as the garden survives, it will be a never-ending annual cycle of making compost and mulching, and giving back to the soil what we take out. I believe making the soil as healthy as possible in an organic way gives the plants the best possible defence against pests, diseases and a drier climate.

So, where to from here? I'm constantly dreaming up new projects – a grass amphitheatre below the pool borders, an ornamental pond and dining pavilion in the already levelled space at the end of the lilac walk, or finding the resources and method to stop our lake leaking, and planting its fringe with a wealth of flowering water plants. Money, water and skills are what are preventing any of these dreams from turning into reality, and that's okay. After all, how big a garden do you need to be happy, although it's great to dream and, every now and then, make one of these dreams come true. Stonefields already gives me a deep sense of achievement and satisfaction, and for the time being – and maybe for all time – this is enough.

I love living by its seasons – if only summer was shorter, and winter longer and wetter, it would be perfect.

I keep thinking of famous garden owners such as Christopher Lloyd at Great Dixter, Vita Sackville-West at Sissinghurst and even our own Dame Elisabeth Murdoch at Cruden Farm, who all shaped their own very personal places. They loved and tended their gardens for decades, and saw out their lives there, nurtured by their creations. Perhaps this is my destiny at Stonefields, as both a gardener and a designer, and there's a lot to be said for it.

OPPOSITE The apple walk in spring, with the 'Crimson Crisp' apple trees in flower. The champagne house is clothed in wisteria.

MAP

1 Lower pool borders
2 Table and Chinese elms
3 Pool garden
4 Herb garden
5 Tank
6 Shed
7 Vegetable garden
8 Apple walk
9 Rose garden
10 Blue borders
11 Entry courtyard
12 Obelisk
13 White garden
14 Caterpillar hedge
15 Drive
16 Studio
17 Tapestry hedge
18 Parterres
19 Woodland
20 Pergola
21 Lilac walk
22 Woodland walk

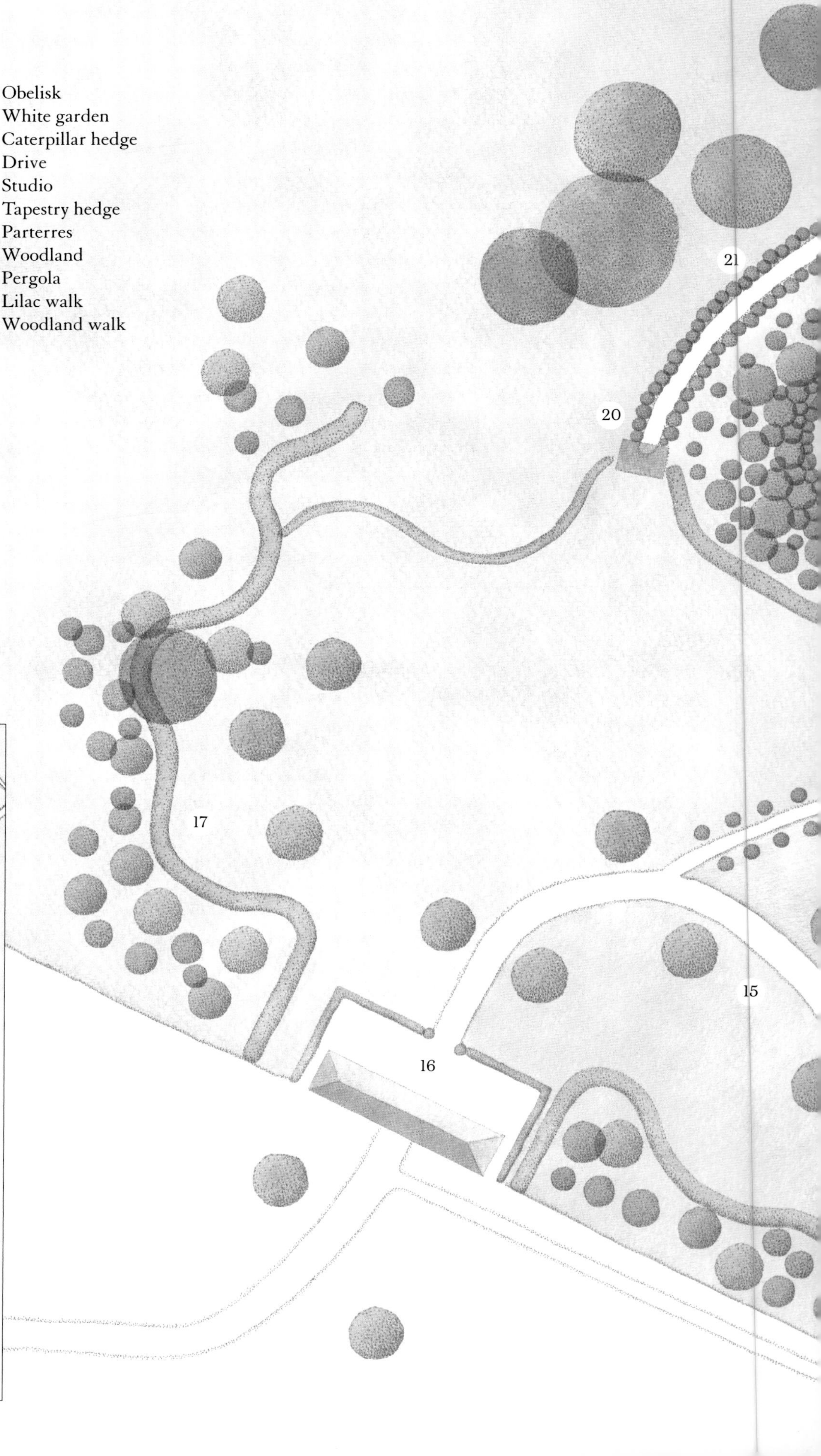

Aerial view showing the farmhouse

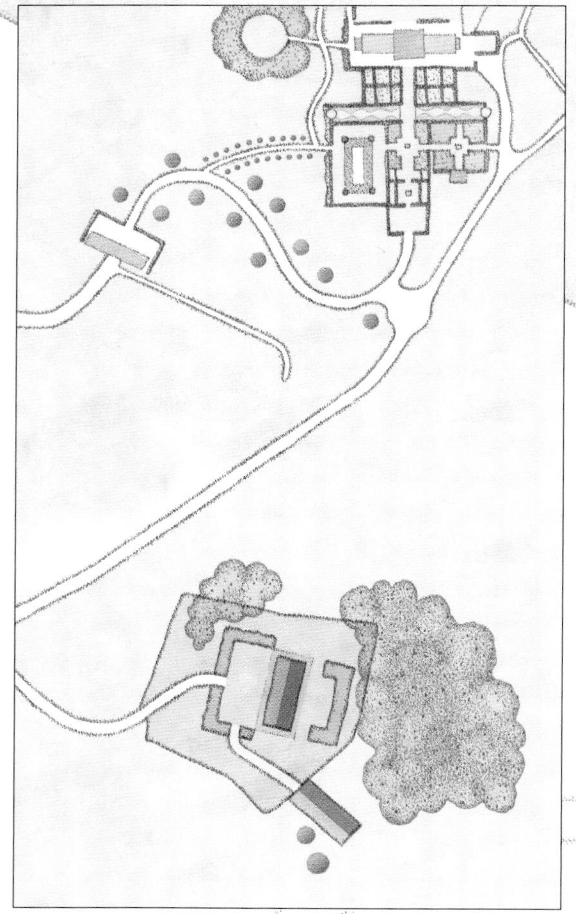

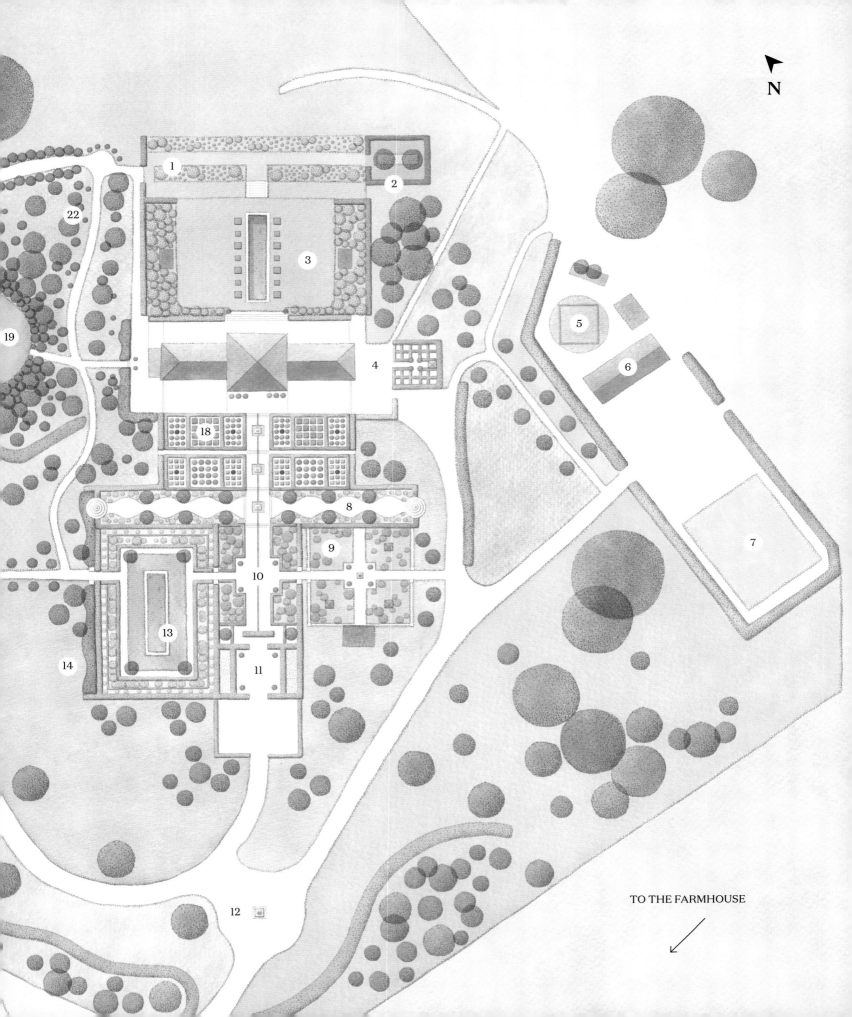

N

1

2

22

3

19

4

5

6

18

7

8

9

10

13

14

11

12

TO THE FARMHOUSE

INDEX

Pages in italics denote photographs

A

Acer truncatum x *platanoides* 'Pacific
    Sunset' *76*, 84, *85*, 118
        autumnal colour *26–7*, *33*, 58
Achillea 'Antique Parchment' 258
Agapanthus campanulatus 'Isis' 259
Agastache 'Blue Boa' 194, *204–5*, *208*,
    224, 258, *259*
Agastache 'Blue Fortune' *74–5*, 194,
    200–1, 258
Agastache 'Sweet Lili' *71*, *74–5*, 194,
    224, 258, *259*
Algerian oaks 233
Allium 'Purple Rain' 72, 158, *160–1*
        borders *162–3*
alliums *162–3*, 195
Anemone x *hybrida* (Japanese
    windflower) 112, 190
Anthemis 'Susannah Mitchell'
    (Marguerite daisy) 194
Anthriscus sylvestris (Raven's wing)
    70, 195, 213
apple walk *182–3*, *186–7*
        in fruit *240–1*
        hedges *168–9*
        in spring *159*, *263*
        in summer *210–1*
Aquilegia vulgaris 'Ruby Port'
    (Columbine) 195, 213
artichokes *121*
Aruncus 195
Aster lateriflorus 'Lady in Black' 50
Aster x *frikartii* 'Jungfrau' 84
Aster x *frikartii* 'Mönch' *74–5*, 84, *224*
Astilbe 195
autumn
        flowering perennials 50–1
        perennial beds 23–4
        plants 84
        pool borders 40–1
        reflection on state of garden 28–9
        tasks 82–3
        trees to plant for colour 58–9
        bulbs to plant 66–73

B

bay (*Laurus nobilis*) 132, 167
berry growing and frames 250
'Bishop of Llandaff' dahlia
    29, *39*, 50, *55*
blue borders 28, 72, *74–5*, *182–3*
        in spring 158, *162–3*, *164–5*,
            194, 195
        in summer *200–1*, *204–5*, *231*
        in winter *90–1*
bluebells *72–3*, *73*, 194
borders
        alliums *162–3*
        hedges *170–1*
        in spring 158
        tulips *164–5*
see also blue borders; perennial beds;
    pool borders
Boston ivy *see Parthenocissus*
    tricuspidata (Boston ivy)
box (*Buxus*)
        effectiveness as hedge 166
        pruning and trimming 82, 193
        susceptibility to mites 29
        see also Buxus sempervirens
            (English box)
broccoli *252*
Brown, Capability 131
bulbs *see* bluebells; daffodils; tulips
burnets *see Sanguisorba*; *Sanguisorba*
    'Cangshan Cranberry'
bushfires 93
        fire retardant strategies 209, 261
Buxus sempervirens (English box)
        cubes *42–3*, *80–1*
        spheres *80–1*, *168–9*
        trimming 257
        in winter *88*, *96–7*

C

Calamagrostis x *acutiflora* 'Karl
    Foerster' *39*, *41*, *216–7*, 258
canker 167
capital works, ideal time for 131
Carpinus betulus see hornbeam
Carpenteria californica (Tree
    anemone) 112
Catmint (*Nepeta* 'Dropmore') 258

Central Highlands of Victoria 16
        bushfire prevalence 209
Ceratostigma willmottianum
    (Chinese plumbago) 50, 77, 84,
    187, 258
charity biennial garden weekend
    137, 191
Chimonanthus praecox (Winter
    sweet) 116, 132
Chinese elm (*Ulmus parvifolia*) 47, *218*
Chinese plumbago (*Ceratostigma*
    willmottianum) 50, 77, 84, 187, 258
'Clearwater' tulips 70, 152, *156–7*,
    176–7, *192*
Clematis 194
Clematis armandii 'Apple Blossom' *184*
Clematis 'Golden Tiara' 40, *44–5*, *243*
climate change and plant
    considerations 158, 261
climbers *see Parthenocissus*
    tricuspidata (Boston ivy); *Vitis*
    coignetiae (Crimson glory vine);
    Wisteria sinensis
cloche for vegetable garden *109*
Columbine (*Aquilegia vulgaris*
    'Ruby Port') 195, 213
composting 82, 193, 261–2
Cornus 'Constellation' (Dogwood)
    143, 195
Cotinus coggygria (Smoke bush) *38*
Cotoneaster horizontalis *41*, 84, *246–7*
crab apple trees *148–51*
        see also Malus x *atrosanguinea*
            'Gorgeous'; *Malus floribunda*;
            Malus spectabilis; *Malus*
            trilobata
Crataegus phaenopyrum (Washington
    thorn) *60–1*, 78
Crimson glory vine *see Vitis*
    coignetiae (Crimson glory vine)
crocus 132
Cruden Farm 262
cubes: English box *44–5*, *80–1*
Culver's root (*Veronicastrum*
    virginicum) 259
Cupressus leylandii 'Leightons
    Green' 167
cut flowers 54
        dogwoods (*Cornus*) 195
        lilacs 187
        roses 56, 213

ACKNOWLEDGEMENTS

Tim and Remi for looking after the garden so well.

Karen Moore for looking after the house and keeping us in line.

Barry for all his amazing love, food and shared belief and interest in Stonefields.

Leta Keens for all her support with my words and thoughts.

Evi O for her amazing art direction.

Isabelle Yates for believing in Stonefields, myself and for allowing us to create this book.

Belinda Handley for all her plant knowledge.

My brother Kent, who always makes everything happen.

Simon Griffiths for his endless support with all things photography and my gardens.

LANTERN

UK | USA | Canada | Ireland | Australia
India | New Zealand | South Africa | China

Lantern is part of the Penguin Random House group of companies whose
addresses can be found at global.penguinrandomhouse.com.

First published by Lantern 2020

Design by Evi-O.Studio | Nicole Ho
© Penguin Random House Australia Pty Ltd
Illustration by Evi-O.Studio | Susan Le
Photography by Simon Griffiths
Edited by Leta Keens

Printed and bound by RR Donnelley Asia Printing Solutions Ltd

ISBN 978 1 76089 508 2

penguin.com.au